Classic WOODEN YACHTS of the Northwest

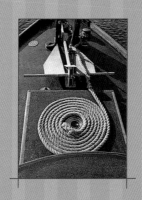

Classic WOODEN YACHTS *of the* Northwest

RON McCLURE

SASQUATCH BOOKS
SEATTLE

CONTENTS

For Kathy

ACKNOWLEDGMENTS

*In compiling the descriptions of the boats presented in this book,
I tried to include at least some of the lore that follows them. Like any oral history retold
over several generations, these stories will be full of gauzy details and opaque points.
Yet these stories are part of the boats, as much as is the paint or varnish topside or oakum
between the planks. The stories came by phone, by email, by letter, and often by casual
conversations with owners as we walked down docks in the Northwest rain. I hope I have
recounted them with reasonable accuracy. Each of the individual accounts went back to
the respective owners for final review and suggestions before the book went to press.*

*I could not have assembled this book without the kindness of the owners,
who spent money on phone calls and sent letters providing histories, photographs,
and memorabilia. Ultimately, each owner graciously allowed me to enter and
photograph their private sanctuary. I thank them all and admire them for their
commitment to the restoration and preservation of fine old wooden boats.
This book is dedicated to people everywhere who own and love wooden boats.*

*I especially thank the following people for their advice,
encouragement, and foresight: Stephen Wilen, Jim Payton, Norm Manly,
John Maag, Joan Gregory, and Karen Schober.*

INTRODUCTION

MY INITIAL CONCEPT IN CREATING this book was to show readers some of the antiquated grandeur I have been lucky enough to witness over the years. However, as I interviewed and photographed, the purpose evolved into something much more. I began to understand and admire not only the beautiful classic wooden boats that grace these pages, but also the dedication, the commitment, the sacrifices of the owners who stand watch over them until it is time to pass them on. As you turn these pages and savor the peeks and glimpses of decks above and cabins below, consider the sacrifices made by the owners who take it upon themselves to see some aging but stately vessel through another decade in a world that has little interest in such nonsense. Notice how the testimonies and the stories that follow all strike a similar theme: People fall in love with some marvelous old beauty or potential beauty. They spend a certain portion of their lives, their money, their passion, and their dreams restoring and preserving her before agreeing to pass their boat on to the next generation. Eventually every classic yacht in this book will need new dreamers to carry her through another century. Perhaps some of those dreamers are reading this very page.

What defines the term "classic wooden motor yacht"? Is it the boat's age? Her lines? The materials she is made of? What makes one boat a classic and another boat just old? Are there authoritative answers to such questions, and if so, does everyone who owns a classic yacht agree with the answers? Or is "classic yacht" a term like "classic rock"—nebulous at best?

Actually, there are accepted answers to these questions. The term generally refers to pre–World War II pleasure craft made of wood that have somehow survived intact, still adhering to their original concept, design, and function. This criteria originated with the Classic Yacht Association, founded in California in 1970 for the purpose of encouraging preservation, restoration, and ongoing maintenance of fine old power-driven pleasure boats. Their qualifications were that the vessel be built prior to 1942, be of good design and construction, be well maintained, and suffer no external alterations that would detract from the designer's original intent. Today this association, with regional chapters stretching from southern California to Alaska, from Rhode Island to Florida, includes more than five hundred classic vessels.

You'll find that the boats showcased in this book all fit the above criteria for classic motor yachts. In addition, these are boats that call the inland and coastal waters of the Pacific Northwest their home. Most were designed and built here, many by the region's foremost designers and boatyards. And each is an example of a "dream afloat"—an antique vessel that somehow inspired dedicated people over the years to invest themselves and their dreams into keeping her alive. The testimonies, recollections, and individual sagas told by the people associated with these boats will give you some insight into just *how* these "dreams afloat" have survived over so many decades.

TACONITE

GORDON LEVETT & LINDA MURRAY *Vancouver, British Columbia*

PERHAPS NO CLASSIC WOODEN CRUISER still plying the waters of the Pacific Northwest embodies more graciously and elegantly the concept of "dreams afloat" than *Taconite*. Built in 1930 by Boeing Aircraft of Canada, Limited, *Taconite* has a hull of four-inch teak planking over cypress frames. She is one hundred twenty-five feet long, twenty-four feet wide, and powered by two Atlas diesel engines that were installed in 1938. Her gross displacement measurement is two hundred eighty-nine tons. Originally conceived by William E. Boeing, Sr., as a floating summer palace for his family, *Taconite* is still serving much the same purpose for her current owners, Gordon Levett and Linda Murray.

Boeing, one of the great industrial giants of the early twentieth century, expanded his Washington-based aircraft company to Canada in 1929 by purchasing the Vancouver shipbuilding company Hoffar-Beeching. Boeing's initial concept was to build seaplanes in

conjunction with the yachts, ferries, and fishing boats that Henry Hoffar was building; however, his plans quickly expanded to the construction of pleasure yachts, including boats such as *Deerleap*, *Willobee G*, *Bardick*, *Cora Marie*, and eventually *Taconite*. (The name *Taconite*, after the iron ore, is a nod to Boeing's years in mining development before he became an aircraft manufacturer.)

For *Taconite*'s construction, Boeing imported the finest materials, including exotic woods from the South Seas such as Burmese teak and Australian eucalyptus. The project, overseen by naval architects Gilbert Jukes and Tom Halliday, employed more than seventy-five Canadian workers for a solid year. The *Taconite* would become the summer home for the Boeing family and the pride of Mrs. Boeing, who loved cruising the waters between Seattle and Alaska.

Unique for her day, *Taconite* embodied elegance, innovation, comfort, and cruising functionality. She was one of the first boats built to include forced-air ventilation. Originally, she had her own communications cabin and a full-time radio operator; eventually, when two-way voice radios were invented, she had one of the first units installed in her pilothouse, eliminating the need for the Morse code operator. (She is also reputed to be the first civilian yacht after World War II to have had radar.) Her interior was a blend of spacious living comfort and the elegance typical of a family as wealthy and successful as the Boeings.

"When I purchased *Taconite* in 1987," says Levett, "I fully understood the enormous responsibility of owning such an important piece of Canadian history and what it would take to restore and maintain the boat to the same degree of perfection as the Boeing family had for nearly half a century."

For Levett, this responsibility has entailed both a commitment and a prodigious investment. He began in 1992 by building a huge floating steel-and-concrete boathouse one hundred fifty feet long and forty-six feet high to protect *Taconite* from the harsh Northwest winters, as well as a one-hundred-sixty-foot outside berth for the boat during the milder seasons.

Levett was committed to keeping *Taconite* original in every way, from her top decks to the engine room. She had had only one other owner since the Boeing family, so fortunately very little had been changed; interior furnishings and the 1930s decor were exactly as they were when the Boeing family cruised the boat to Alaska every summer.

Levett's first major task was to begin the restoration of *Taconite*'s teak decks. The previous owner had painted the decks and much of the

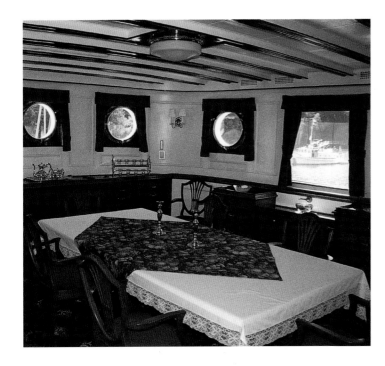

solid teak brightwork, so Levett began the endless process of removing all of the paint, recaulking the deck seams, and replacing the screws. It took over eight thousand four-inch bronze screws and some eleven thousand ⅝-inch teak plugs.

Levett modified the boat's original mechanical design by installing a system that lets him control the engines from the pilothouse. In the original setup, typical of large boats of that period, engine operation was carried out by telegraph between the captain in the pilothouse and a full-time, experienced engineer in the engine room. With the updated controls, Levett and Murray can operate the boat themselves. (The original system is still in place, however, and still functional.) Docking a one-hundred-twenty-five-foot yacht is a challenge, but they manage just fine, with the aid of a twenty-seven-inch bow thruster that was installed in 1990. It's like having two extra deckhands, Levett notes.

Taconite's 1930s elegance begins in her formal dining room, located forward and just below the pilothouse. The exquisite teak joinery work is lighted by large round port-lights, velvet-draped side windows, and

sterling silver wall sconces. An enclosed passageway leads past her stainless steel galley and large master stateroom to her comfortable and luxurious main salon. This grand living space, complete with wood-burning fireplace, remains today exactly as it was when the Boeings lived aboard during their summer cruises. Many of the same paintings still grace the walls. Sliding teak French doors open to the covered aft deck, Mrs. Boeing's favorite spot, complete with a teak wet bar, cushioned seating that curves around the stern rail, and the original framed, hand-painted charts of the British Columbia coastline, dating from 1931.

Boeing was a perfectionist, and *Taconite* reflects that in every possible way. He kept a full-time crew of ten on the boat year-round, and they logged in detail every repair, item of maintenance, or improvement. The Boeing family cruised *Taconite* over 250,000 nautical miles. "We have all of the original pilothouse and engine-room log books from 1930 to the present—over two hundred of them," Levett says.

Part of Levett's commitment includes rebuilding *Taconite*'s massive Atlas diesels, weighing sixteen tons each. Although the engines operated perfectly when he purchased the boat, Levett decided in 1994 that both were due for an overhaul eventually if extended Inside Passage cruising was to continue. The Atlas company has gone out of business and few parts are available anywhere, so almost every nut, bolt, and gasket must be refabricated, with precisely the same materials as the originals. Levett has purchased any available new parts to keep as spares, in addition to purchasing three complete used engines. The spare parts alone fill up a forty-foot trailer warehouse.

"It's quite an undertaking," says Levett. "We completed the rebuild on the starboard engine in 1994 and plan to overhaul the port engine in the year 2000."

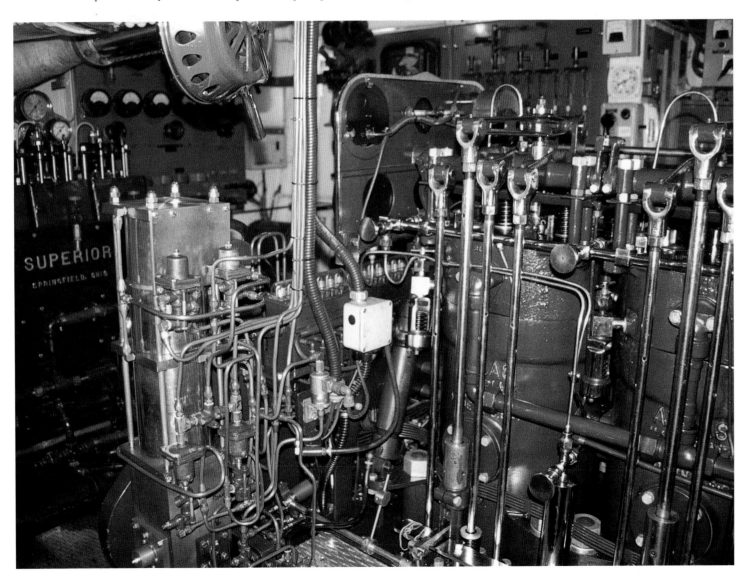

Taconite's home port has always been Vancouver, British Columbia. She is very much a part of the history of Canada and the Inside Passage to Alaska. Levett and Murray's commitment to this surviving historical link speaks in its own way for the commitment of everyone involved in preserving classic wooden boats. Like the great forests these boats were created from, once lost, they are forever gone. No imagination or technological innovation will ever bring them back. It is only the resolve of owners today that ensures their continued existence.

TACONITE

Year: 1930

Designer: Tom Halliday

Builder: Boeing Aircraft of Canada, Limited,
Vancouver, British Columbia

Length: 125 feet

Beam: 24 feet

Draft: 9 feet

Original Power: Twin Wintons

Current Power: Twin Atlas (diesel)

Construction: Burmese teak over cypress frames.

Home Port: Vancouver, British Columbia

HAIDA PRINCESS

MIKE & PEGGY O'BRIEN *North Vancouver, British Columbia*

IT WAS THE SUMMER OF 1974, and Mike and Peggy O'Brien were tied up at a dock on one of Canada's Gulf Islands. Peggy was stitching cushion covers, Mike was sanding. Suddenly, Mike recalls, they had a life-changing experience. "Two marvelous teak and mahogany cruisers hushed into Bedwell Harbour, side by side. One was the *Cle Illahee* and the other was the *Euphemia*. From that day forward, our mission in life became finding a classic yacht."

That quest eventually led Mike to a rain-soaked boatyard in North Vancouver, where he discovered *Haida Princess*—up on blocks, surrounded by piles of fishnets and boat parts. Eight or ten coats of white house paint covered every inch of her, including her gorgeous hardwood floors and teak interior, and to top it all off, the plumber who owned her had plumbing fixtures screwed or bolted onto every available surface. But once the O'Briens saw her back in the water and were able to appreciate her gorgeous lines, there was

never any question. *Haida Princess* was the boat they had been searching for.

"We spent the next six years basically following the same routine. I would pick up the roasted chicken on my way home from work on Friday afternoons. We would spend Friday night, Saturday, and most of Sunday on the boat scraping, sanding, varnishing our hearts out, and doing the ten thousand things that wooden boat lovers do to revive a once beautiful little ship."

For *Haida Princess*, this love's labor included replacing some thirty-six ribs, various planks, and virtually all of the wood in the transom—as well as removing the many layers of white paint and filling all the screw holes before sanding and varnishing her beautiful teak joinery work.

Haida Princess's layout is one of a kind. The unique forward cabin is a combination sleeping compartment and lounging/dining area,

with a compact galley. Half-bulkheads maintain a feeling of separation between these areas. Gloss-white walls, a polished teak skylight and chain locker door, 1920s bronze and opaque lamps, and varnished hardwood floors all speak eloquently of the care that has gone into her restoration.

Unusual in an early 1920s yacht is the inclusion of a completely separate sleeping compartment aft, accessible from the steering station by a companionway. The interior of the aft cabin is deep and private, with solid varnished teak, extensive storage drawers, and polished brass hardware.

Her "wheelhouse" is actually a covered steering station, yet the canvas and transparent side curtains keep weather out, protecting the varnished teak, distinctive bronze control levers, binnacle, and pedestal steering column.

Her logbooks show that *Haida Princess* has circumnavigated Vancouver Island six times. From 1935 to 1978, she was owned by a dentist from Maple Falls, on Vancouver Island, known as Doc Qually. During the war years it was impossible to get gas for pleasure boating.

Mike O'Brien tells of the deal Qually cut with the Canadian government. "He mounted a dental chair in his wheelhouse and spent his summers cruising up and down the B.C. coast on Canadian government gas, stopping at logging camps to yank out teeth."

Haida Princess was partly built by a Vancouver sash-and-door contractor named R. D. Helmer. Helmer wanted a stout little cruiser to transport himself and his family between the city and their summer home, north of Vancouver on Howe Sound. He had the hull constructed at the Hoffar-Beeching yard and then finished the boat himself at his shop. With her original Sterling six-cylinder gas engine,

installed by Hoffar-Beeching, she could make fifteen knots—a fast cruising boat for its time.

"Can you imagine what it must have been like, owning a little yacht like this back in 1925?" Mike O'Brien reflects. "Cruising her all the way to Howe Sound with your family aboard? That was the era of silent films. Chaplin's *Gold Rush* was playing in movie houses. It was ten years before the invention of the jet engine, really before the age of flight by today's standards. That was truly elegant living."

Today *Haida Princess* is once again elegant, thanks to the dreams and efforts of her dedicated owners.

HAIDA PRINCESS

Year: 1925
Designer: Unknown
Builder: R. D. Helmer, Vancouver, British Columbia
Length: 36 feet
Beam: 9 feet 6 inches
Draft: 3 feet 6 inches
Original Power: Sterling
Current Power: Volvo TMD-30 (diesel)
Construction: Cedar on oak frames. Teak decks and cabins.
Home Port: North Vancouver, British Columbia

WAHOMA

MONTY & SHIRLEE HOLMES *Seattle, Washington*

THE BOATING INDUSTRY IN THE PACIFIC NORTHWEST owes an enormous debt to the influence of Ed Monk, Sr. Examples of his designs are afloat today in nearly every Northwest harbor, moorage, and anchorage, whether they are commercial fishing boats, one-of-a-kind classic motor yachts, production pleasure craft, or graceful sailboats. Monk is one of the undisputed fathers of the classic bridge-deck cruiser, and certainly one of the most important contributors to the liveaboard concept in small yachts. *Wahoma* is one of the finest surviving examples of the Monk legacy.

Monk himself was a liveaboard, and roominess is a Monk hallmark. Unlike some classics, which offer "standing room only" in the pilothouse, *Wahoma* has a large, comfortable settee abaft the steering station, fronted by a long chart table/serving table, allowing passengers to ride in comfort while enjoying the same panoramic view as the captain. Her forward stateroom, with single berths to port and starboard, has full headroom and plenty of dressing space.

Prewar classics are traditionally narrow, often with beam widths of between nine and eleven feet. *Wahoma*, sporting a beam of thirteen feet nine inches, again attests to Monk's liveaboard experience. Her unusually spacious main cabin contains two large dinette booths, each capable of seating up to six persons. Abaft the dinettes are a head to port and a full shower to starboard. Her large galley, forward of the seating area, easily provides working space for two people. All of this living, cooking, and gathering space in one cabin is truly unusual in prewar classic cruisers.

Wahoma was built in 1939, when a University of Washington geologist, J. B. Umpleby, commissioned Lake Washington Boat Works in Seattle to create a fifty-foot bridge-deck cruiser designed by Monk. Unfortunately, Umpleby had little time to enjoy her because she was taken into service by the U.S. Coast Guard at the outset of World War II. She served as a patrol boat on the Columbia Bar at the mouth of the Columbia River, where the seas create some of the most treacherous waters on the West Coast. According to an article by Michael Dunatov in the January 1988 issue of *Waterlines*, her performance there was so impressive that the Coast Guard used her design as a prototype for other patrol boats built during the war.

Surplused in 1947, *Wahoma* was purchased by Doc Freeman, founder of Doc Freeman's, Inc., a marine supply house in Seattle. Freeman began her restoration. She was later sold to Gene Walby, owner of an athletic supply company, and during the 1950s she played host to many famous coaches and athletes. She spent the next twenty years of her life under cover at Seattle's Queen City Yacht Club. Her logbooks also indicate that she twice circumnavigated Vancouver Island and trekked as far north as Juneau, Alaska, during the early 1950s.

This beautiful boat has been a part of current owner Monty Holmes's life for over fifty years. As a young man, he worked as her caretaker and engineer when Walby owned her. Holmes purchased *Wahoma* from Walby in 1978. Since that time, one of his primary goals has been to keep the boat as completely original as possible, down to the smallest detail. The exquisite care that Holmes and his wife, Shirlee, continue to take in restoring and refurbishing *Wahoma* amazes onlookers who flock to this boat whenever she attends a classic rendezvous. The detail of her exterior brightwork and bronze fittings, her bronze portholes and yellow cedar decks, the flawless condition of her hull, the beauty of her mahogany stern plate with gold lettering—all show a pride of ownership that is rarely surpassed.

WAHOMA

Year: 1939
Designer: Ed Monk, Sr.
Builder: Lake Washington Boat Works, Seattle, Washington
Length: 50 feet
Beam: 13 feet 9 inches
Draft: 5 feet
Original Power: Twin Chrysler Crowns (gas)
Current Power: Same
Construction: Alaskan yellow cedar planking and decks over white oak frames. Mahogany cabin.
Home Port: Seattle, Washington

SHEARWATER

RON & KATHY McCLURE
Anacortes, Washington

THE SAME YEAR THAT RENOWNED Seattle naval architect Ed Monk, Sr., designed *Shearwater*, he designed his own boat, *Nan*. That was in 1933, and Monk and his family lived aboard *Nan* for several years, also using her as an office for Monk's design business. To Monk, interior comfort and practicality were always as vital as other aspects of boat design.

Shearwater is one of the best surviving examples of Monk's fusion of classic motor-yacht lines, superb interior joinery work, and comfortable liveaboard functionality. Her spacious pilothouse affords excellent headroom and 360-degree visibility. Her deep V-hull provides a comfortable, luxurious feeling under way.

The boat's privacy and functionality begin in the forepeak (the extreme forward section of the boat), which houses a chain locker, ample storage shelves, and a large electric windlass motor for hoisting the anchor. The forward head opens to the master stateroom, which contains a raised double berth, with plenty of storage and a seating area between the hanging lockers. Steps lead up to the wheelhouse, with a sizable combination chart table/dining table and bookshelves behind the settee. While the boat is under way, the companionways both forward and aft can be buttoned up with doors and hatch covers.

Steps portside lead aft to a large galley with the original four-burner stove and oven, sink fixtures, cabinetry, and icebox. A long mahogany counter for food preparation has leaded glass cabinet windows above. Beyond the galley is the salon, with a low couch/double-berth conversion, loads of storage, and two full-sized hanging lockers. A unique Monk feature in this boat is the location of the primary head opposite the galley and separated by a center bulkhead running fore and aft. This creates still more privacy and separate living spaces. An early riser can cook breakfast in the aft section of the boat three compartments away from someone who is sleeping in.

My wife, Kathy, and I purchased *Shearwater* in 1997 from Joel Rindal, past commodore of the Queen City Yacht Club in Seattle, who was one of two long-term owners. Her log books show that she had spent most of her life under covered moorage at the Queen City Yacht Club, and she had always been well cared for. She was originally powered by a Hall-Scott Invader six-cylinder gas engine. Rindal repowered the boat during the 1970s with a slightly newer version of the same engine, made during the early 1940s by the Hudson Motor Company.

Shortly after we bought *Shearwater* and while she was in temporary moorage in a marina in Anacortes, Washington, the boat next to her exploded and sank. Severely burned and scarred, *Shearwater* was left sitting in a boatyard waiting to be trucked off to an auction block in Seattle. We were sick.

It is hard to explain why people become involved with a particular wooden boat. Some couples invest more time, money, and effort in restoring an old wooden boat than normal people would invest in buying and maintaining a house. Kathy saw the explosion as a sign that *Shearwater* wanted to be completely restored and repowered to live another sixty-five years, providing both us and her future owners with comfortable and secure cruising.

Since that day, *Shearwater* has undergone extensive restoration stem to stern. The process is ongoing. We installed new glass, removed and renewed paint and varnish, scraped and sanded charred brightwork, and repaired the canvas deck covering. A new John Deere 4045-T diesel replaced the early 1940s Hudson engine. We've refastened and recorked her hull and rebuilt or replaced all her systems.

Today *Shearwater* remains a splendid example of the Monk legacy. The joinery work and superstructure are dark Honduras mahogany.

Her floors are carpeted in dark green and her ceiling ribs capped with varnished mahogany throughout, enhancing an interior lushness of polished brass, chrome, dark mahogany, and early 1930s charm.

Throughout the process of bringing *Shearwater* back to her original elegance, we strove to maintain all of her original design and appearance both inside and out, keeping her true to Monk's vision as well as to the period in which she was built. This attention to original design and period is part of the enjoyment and the challenge of owning a classic motor yacht.

SHEARWATER

Year: 1933

Designer: Ed Monk, Sr.

Builder: Schertzer Boat Works, Seattle, Washington

Length: 45 feet

Beam: 11 feet 6 inches

Draft: 4 feet 4 inches

Original Power: Hall-Scott Invader

Current Power: John Deere 4045-T (diesel)

Construction: Cedar planks over white oak steam-bent frames.

Canvas-covered decks. Honduras mahogany house and salon.

Home Port: Anacortes, Washington

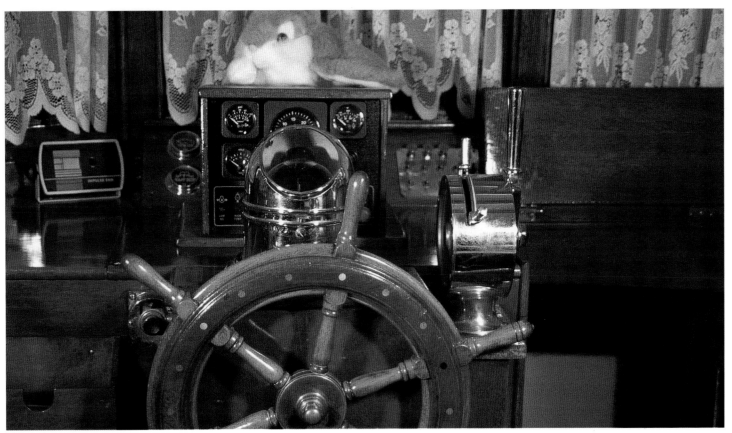

HANNA

DON & SHRYL EATON
Friday Harbor, Washingtonf

BETWEEN THE FIRST AND SECOND WORLD WARS, a number of boat-building companies sprouted along the banks of Seattle's Lake Union. Turning out fishing boats, working boats, and occasionally pleasure boats, they would operate for a few years, and then move away, burn down (not uncommon), or simply disappear.

One such company was Schertzer Boat Works. Located on the north end of Seattle's Lake Union, they apparently disappeared or relocated sometime during the 1930s, but not before creating some of the Northwest's best-known classic yachts, including *Kiyi*, *Rum Runner*, *Shearwater*, *Euphemia*, and *Hanna*.

Hanna, orginally named *Sandpiper II*, was built in 1927 for a man named Stanley Piper. An otherwise standard bridge-deck cruiser with V-berth forward and galley and dinette in the salon, she has one unusual luxury: a glass-enclosed aft cockpit that provides a comfortable and protected area for dining or lounging in cool or rainy weather. In most classics, this "back porch" is open, since it was designed for fishing and deploying the dinghy, and this was originally true of *Hanna*. During World War II, however, she underwent a transformation, when Piper, like many yachtsmen, gave his boat up to the U.S. Coast Guard. Unlike most cruisers, which were painted gray and converted into patrol boats, *Sandpiper II* was used as a review boat. To accommodate Coast Guard officers in the climate of the Pacific Northwest, the service employed a shipwright to turn the open aft cockpit into a glass-enclosed solarium. Fortunately, this addition was done with solid teak, in perfect keeping with the boat's style and design.

Her current owners, Don and Shryl Eaton of Friday Harbor, Washington, had begun a quest for a classic of their own in 1993, when friends invited them on a trip to Desolation Sound aboard the 1927 custom cruiser *Arequipa*. Their search eventually led them to

Bellingham, Washington, where a classic boat owner steered them to Ralph and Hanna French, longtime owners of *Sandpiper II*. The Frenches invited the Eatons to visit them at the Victoria Wooden Boat Festival, and a long relationship began. "Both Hanna French and I knew that we were going to be the *Sandpiper*'s next owners," says Shryl Eaton, "but Ralph felt very differently about it." At the time, he would not even discuss selling his boat.

The Eatons continued their search for three years. Then, in early 1996, they got a phone call. Ralph French was thinking of selling.

"We went to look at the boat in March, when they had her hauled out to paint her bottom. Ralph and Hanna were sitting in their car eating sandwiches, and both were covered from head to toe in paint. Ralph was eighty-one at the time and Hanna was seventy-six."

Although negotiations were started, French was still very attached to his boat. Not long after, however, he suffered a fatal heart attack, and later that spring Hanna French agreed to sell the boat to the Eatons.

The Eatons renamed the boat *Hanna* and spent a year and a half cruising and enjoying her. However, when they had her hauled for

bottom maintenance, they discovered she was in desperate need of hull repairs, including the replacement of nineteen planks and fifty-five new steam-bent oak ribs. And this was only the beginning.

In the following years, *Hanna* underwent major restoration. The Eatons installed new fuel tanks, rebuilt the transom, put in a new rudder post, completely refastened the hull, and replaced the plumbing systems and the engine. This very process is the reason *Hanna* will go on and on—outliving both the company that built her and the generations who have owned and loved her.

HANNA

Year: 1927
Designer: Unknown
Builder: Schertzer Boat Works, Seattle, Washington
Length: 38 feet
Beam: 9 feet
Draft: 3 feet 4 inches
Original Power: Kermath
Current Power: Not installed at press time
Construction: Red cedar on oak. Teak cabins.
Home Port: Friday Harbor, Washington

MAHAR

RON & LYNN RENDER *Poulsbo, Washington*

IT'S HARD TO BELIEVE *Mahar* was homemade. From the graceful canoe shape of her stern and the exquisite joinery work of her superstructure, any observer would assume that this trim double-ender, designed in the classic bridge-deck tradition, came out of a professional boatyard. Yet *Mahar*, built in Victoria, British Columbia, between 1931 and 1934, was entirely the work of a nonprofessional named Harold Campbell, with the help of his family and friends.

During the thirties, forties, and fifties, *Mahar* changed owners many times. Eventually she was acquired by Paul Hosea, a boatwright on Lake Union in Seattle, who spent eighteen years cruising, restoring, and rebuilding her.

Powered by a Perkins diesel, *Mahar* now boasts updated electronics, plumbing, and head facilities as well as a functionally enhanced galley. Yet despite these modern improvements, she appears little changed from when she was built. Her pilothouse is a beautiful blend of original brass and bronze hardware, exotic varnished woods, and modern electrical switches and gauges. The restoration of her mahogany superstructure is as gorgeous outside as inside. Her cabin sides, doors, pilothouse windows, and toe rails are detailed to the finest degree. The exterior bronze hardware is polished to a golden mirror finish, and her canvas-covered decks are impeccable.

Ron and Lynn Render acquired the boat "quite by happenstance." Returning from the Victoria Classic Boat Festival, they spotted her on Lake Union with a For Sale sign. "We had no plans to purchase a forty-foot bridge-deck cruiser, but her classic lines and extraordinary condition outweighed any rational thought," says Lynn Render. At some point the boat had been renamed *Sandalo,* but as soon as they bought her the Renders returned her original name—derived from the names of her first owners, *Ma*y and *Har*old Campbell.

Mahar is a very comfortable boat for cruising. She has a deep hull and a long keel, allowing her to track well in a seaway and to handle the frequent tide rips and stong currents encountered in Pacific Northwest waters.

The Renders live the dream of every classic enthusiast by enjoying their boat just as she was designed to be enjoyed—living aboard for much of the summer while exploring the San Juan Islands of northwest Washington or the Gulf Islands of British Columbia, anchoring in the many small coves or marine parks that dot the region. But although cruising is their main pursuit, preservation is equally important to them. "We spend part of nearly every day on board maintaining her," says Lynn Render. "We will continue this process until she is turned over to her next stewards."

MAHAR

Year: 1934

Designer: Unknown

Builder: Harold Campbell, Victoria, British Columbia

Length: 40 feet

Beam: 11 feet 8 inches

Draft: 4 feet 6 inches

Original Power: Junker

Current Power: Perkins 6-354 (diesel)

Construction: Yellow cedar planking over white oak frames.

Mahogany house.

Home Port: Poulsbo, Washington

CHARLES H. CATES

EARL DAVID & SUZANNE CATES DODSON *North Vancouver, British Columbia*

FOR WHAT THEY'VE SPENT on restoring their old wooden boat, Earl and Suzanne Dodson know they could easily have purchased a brand-new modern yacht twice its size, with all the amenities. But "every cent we've spent was worth it," maintains Suzanne Dodson with considerable pride. The restoration of their boat is much more than just a "labor of love" to this dedicated couple. It's a tribute to Suzanne Dodson's father, Charles W. Cates, and to her grandfather, Charles H. Cates.

Vancouver, British Columbia, is one of the busiest commercial shipping ports in North America, and the C. H. Cates and Sons tugboat company of North Vancouver has always been at the core of this activity. Founded by Charles H. Cates shortly before the turn of the century, the company remained in the family until 1992. Charles W. Cates was one of the three sons who took over the company. The *Charles H. Cates* was built in 1913 as a company pleasure craft and remained in that capacity for almost fifty years. Her original name was *Gaviota*, the Spanish word for "seagull."

Suzanne Dodson remembers countless excursions on the company boat as a little girl with her father. However, after her father died in 1960, the boat sat inactive. Then in 1992 she heard by chance that *Gaviota* was for sale by the new owners of the Cates tugboat company. She and her husband were able to purchase "Gavie" and to begin the task of total restoration.

And what a task. Over the decades, *Charles H. Cates* had not only deteriorated badly but had undergone considerable changes to her superstructure and interior. The Dodsons began by studying old photos and by examining the original woods, most of which had been covered with plywood or painted over. Then they completely replanked the hull with old-growth Western red cedar from Vancouver Island. Every rib was sistered or replaced. Her decks were

relaid with Douglas fir, and she was given a new stem, stern post, and toe rails of gumwood. Her superstructure, too, is entirely new. "The keel is still original," observes Earl Dodson, wryly.

"We found a shipwright named Fred Amor who was really the man responsible for Gavie's rebirth," says Suzanne Dodson. "Without his belief and his abilities in the project, it could never have happened."

As you step onto *Charles H. Cates* today, you would never suspect that she was originally built in 1913 and had gone through years of deterioration. The joinery work in the cockpit, the exterior brightwork, the smooth, canvas-covered decks are pristine. The covered cockpit and steering station easily seats four, with plenty of room for the captain.

Below decks, a sparkling galley is immediately to port. Her engine box doubles as a table, with seating on either side. The head and hanging locker are located between the main salon and the forward sleeping cabin. The interior, complemented with polished brass fixtures, is finished in attractive yellow cedar and teak.

You might also be impressed by the boat's stoutness. Away from the docks, she feels as if she had been designed as much for work as for pleasure, and Earl Dodson says she has all of his confidence in rough weather.

"We bought the boat because the Cates Company was my father's entire life," says Suzanne Dodson. "Keeping her and restoring her to perfection is a tribute to his love for his work and for the company."

CHARLES H. CATES

Year: 1913
Designer: Andrew Linton
Builder: Andrew Linton, North Vancouver, British Columbia
Length: 38 feet
Beam: 9 feet
Draft: 4 feet
Original Power: Vivian
Current Power: Bedford Vauxhall (diesel)
Construction: Douglas fir keel. Old-growth Western red cedar carvel-planked over oak frames. Douglas fir decks.
Home Port: North Vancouver, British Columbia

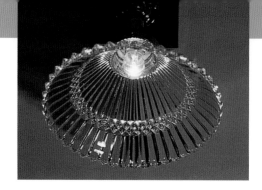

MER-NA

MARTY LOKEN & GLORIA GRANDAW, *Seattle, Washington*

WHAT TYPE OF CLASSIC WOODEN CRUISER would someone choose if they owned a wooden boat restoration shop—or better yet, a wooden boat store? Marty Loken owns both, and his choice for the past fourteen years has been the thirty-six-foot Blanchard *Mer-Na*.

"We got bit back in 1980," Loken remembers, "when we chartered another full-sized cruiser, *Sunrise New York,* for a week. Before that we had always owned smaller boats. At the time *Mer-Na* belonged to a friend of ours, so I already knew the boat and knew the excellent shape she was in." *Mer-Na* had spent virtually her entire life under cover at Seattle's Queen City Yacht Club. One previous owner had kept her for thirty-five years, and Loken is sure she was always professionally maintained. "After the cruise, we knew that a boat like *Mer-Na* was exactly what we wanted."

But *Mer-Na* wasn't available. For six years, Loken and his wife,

Gloria Grandaw, "watched this little boat like vultures." Finally, their vigilance was rewarded: She came up for sale.

Mer-Na is a marvelous example of designer Leigh Coolidge's concept of a functional yet comfortable cruiser. The layout of the Blanchard 36 is being copied in cruisers to this day. The fairly roomy forward cabin has a V-berth, with storage drawers below, dressing area, and half-door access to the chain locker. Aft of the sleeping compartment are a hanging locker and an enclosed head to starboard, and the galley to port. The main salon contains opposing settees that can be converted into four single bunks. A center companionway leads up to the steering station, with hatch access to the engine compartment beneath the wheelhouse.

Loken's professional attention to detail and his restoration expertise have served *Mer-Na* well. She retains all of her original fixtures— her porcelain-coated Lang kerosene galley stove, her lighting, even

her original bronze plumbing lines. At one time her Kermath engine had been replaced by a massive Chrysler Royal 145-horsepower engine, but Loken has repowered her with a Yanmar four-cylinder diesel.

For Loken, stewardship is the key concept with a classic like *Mer-Na*.

"I've had several smaller boats that I've felt I actually *owned*. But a classic cruiser is different. You don't *own* these things, you merely take care of them—preserve and maintain them till you pass them along to the next generation of boaters."

The quality of the boats he sees at classic rendezvous and wooden boat shows is continually improving, Loken says. "The boats are being maintained to higher standards because now people are starting to realize how important they are. People have gained a deeper appreciation of their design and functionality." His Blanchard 36 is eloquent testimony to this appreciation.

MER-NA

Year: 1930
Designer: Leigh Coolidge
Builder: Blanchard Boat Company, Seattle, Washington
Length: 36 feet
Beam: 9 feet 6 inches
Draft: 3 feet 5 inches
Original Power: Kermath
Current Power: Yanmar (diesel)
Construction: Western red cedar. White oak frames. Teak house.
Home Port: Seattle, Washington

FAUN

MICHAEL PASSAGE & LAURA STONE SHIFFLETTE
Seattle, Washington

"I THINK OUR FIRST ADDITION to *Faun* was the geraniums," says Laura Stone Shifflette. "Of course, it took a lot more than just flowers."

Shifflette and co-owner Michael Passage discovered *Faun* at the 1997 Bell Street Pier Classic Rendezvous in Seattle, the largest gathering of prewar classic cruisers on the West Coast. In 1999, their boat won the People's Choice Award at the same festival.

"We had no intentions or expectations whatsoever of buying a boat," says Shifflette. "In fact, we intended not to buy a boat, but when we saw *Faun*, it was truly love at first sight."

It's easy to see why *Faun* would be voted the People's Choice at any festival she attends. The exterior teak of her cabin, deep-toned and beautifully grained, invites touch as though it were the back of a guitar. Her original brass port-lights and deck hardware glisten as though they were newly minted. Her hull, aft swim step, stern plate, and foredeck are all detailed to perfection.

Faun's extended aft cabin, which was not enclosed in the original design, is even more striking, with flowers, Oriental carpets, and period-appropriate wicker furniture. Polished brass and bronze fixtures shine against beautifully refinished teak. Her spacious galley, with the original Neptune stove converted to kerosene, is a perfect blend of antique charm and updated functionality—from the stainless steel stovepipe to the addition of a small, discreetly placed microwave oven.

Built in 1926 and selling new for $6,000, *Faun* is one of the surviving Blanchard Standardized Cruisers, built by Norman J. Blanchard's company to take advantage of the growing market for affordable motor yachts. The Blanchard Boat Company, which was located on Lake Union in Seattle, was an industry forerunner in developing a line of small production cruisers for the rapidly growing pleasure craft market of the Roaring Twenties. These comfortable and practical

boats were an early departure from the one-of-a-kind custom yachts commissioned by the very wealthy.

Faun's original engine was a Van Blerk, replaced in 1946 by the current Chrysler Crown six-cylinder gas. During World War II, *Faun* was commissioned by the Navy as an officer's launch and painted gray. Her interior was refitted in 1991 and her exterior restored in 1997.

Since they purchased *Faun*, Shifflette and Passage have completely wooded, grooved, and repainted her hull. While her brightwork was being revarnished, nearly all the metal parts were removed and profes-

sionally recoated and polished. Throughout the restoration, they paid strict attention to maintaining the boat's original character and design.

"We found a postcard in an old bookstore," says Shifflette. "It pictured the Victoria Classic Boat Festival, taken about twenty years ago. Right in the center of the picture is *Faun*. We've used that postcard as a reference in restoring the boat."

Shifflette loves the "see-through" design of the boat, which makes it possible to stand in the forward cabin and see out through the aft windows. The couple use the boat year-round. During cold weather,

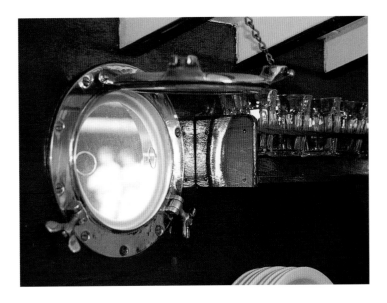

the Neptune stove keeps the entire boat cozy, and in summer they cruise for ten weeks at a time through Washington's San Juans and the Canadian Gulf Islands.

"We often wake up thinking about our boat and all of the things that we want to do with her and the places we want to go. Then we start thinking about all of the months and years of our lives that we wasted on less important things before we owned her—or rather before she owned us."

FAUN

Year: 1926
Designer: Leigh Coolidge
Builder: Blanchard Boat Company, Seattle, Washington
Length: 36 feet
Beam: 9 feet 6 inches
Draft: 3 feet
Original Power: Van Blerk
Current Power: Chrysler Crown (gas)
Construction: Red cedar on white oak frames. Teak house.
Home Port: Seattle, Washington

RITA

LEW & LINDY BARRETT *Seattle, Washington*

BUILT IN 1938 BY ED WHITE of Seattle's Lakewood Boat Company, *Rita* is another superb example of the living legacy of Ed Monk, Sr. Her design clearly reveals why his boats were—and continue to be—so popular.

Monk, one of the premier naval architects of the Pacific Northwest from the late 1920s through the 1960s, designed everything from dinghies to sailboats to powerboats. (During World War II, he even found himself designing military patrol boats, fishing boats, tugs, and towboats.) Yet the Monk legend is connected more with classic power cruisers than with any other style of boat.

Rita has a teak house and interior and three cabins, with a head forward and a second head aft. Her trunk cabin employs a neat keyhole design that separates the galley from the salon area, which holds a settee to starboard and a built-in table to port that seats six. There is a hanging locker aft, opposite the head, and her spacious covered cockpit is wide and deep enough to hold several pieces of wicker furniture. Yet, beyond this simple description, a closer inspection sheds light on why Monk's designs have continued to work so well for cruising enthusiasts.

Rita's galley is easily as large as some apartment kitchens. Monk's concept of spreading the galley across the beam of the boat just behind the pilothouse, where the beam is greatest, provides the initial space. His foresight in locating the main companionway as far to port as possible creates the long counter workspace and sink area against the bulkhead that separates the salon and pilothouse. The stove is tucked into an L-shaped area to starboard, providing enough room for two people to work in the galley at the same time—a rare luxury on classic cruisers. The keyhole concept of separating the galley from the dining area, though by no means a Monk invention, is the most appropriate choice in cruisers like *Rita*. It

provides the feel of separate compartments while creating that attractive openness typical of Monk's "big window" designs.

Most classic cruisers achieve comfortable interior space by omitting exterior side decks. *Rita*'s twelve-foot seven-inch beam, however, provides for side decks with stanchions and handrails, allowing the crew to move fore and aft more safely while handling fenders and lines. Yet this is not a common design attribute of most prewar classics, whose beam seldom exceeded eleven feet.

Rita's current owners, Lew and Lindy Barrett, admit they spent years walking docks, peeking into boathouses, and searching yacht brokerages all over the Northwest before they finally found *Rita* in Bellingham, Washington.

"Everybody I trusted warned me about buying an old wooden boat," Lew Barrett says with amusement, "but she was so beautiful that I couldn't resist, and almost totally original."

Yet, as many classic lovers quickly discover, being "original" can also mean being very tired, and Barrett confesses that he has spent thousands of hours on *Rita*'s restoration. Decks, house, hull, heads, electrical systems, plumbing, tankage, upholstery, stove, furnace, paint, varnish—the

list goes on forever, but in *Rita*'s case the results have clearly been worth the effort. Her bright decks, laid in teak and fir, are a work of varnished art. Her beige hull has a fair surface comparable to many modern fiberglass hulls, and her canvas-covered top decks are equally flawless. The interior bulkheads in the salon and galley have been finished to such perfection that it is hard to believe they are more than sixty years old.

Barrett acknowledges that one of the best features of owning *Rita* is the way she draws people at docks or at boat shows. "That's the thing about owning a classic," he says. "Perhaps it does take a little more time, a little more effort, but it's worth it."

Yet he also points out that *Rita* is much more than just a dockside queen. "We go everywhere in *Rita*. She's been to Desolation Sound, the Gulf Islands, the San Juans of course, and all over Puget Sound. And I've learned never to worry at all. She can really take it."

"Really taking it" is just one more aspect of the Monk legacy.

RITA

Year: 1938
Designer: Ed Monk, Sr.
Builder: Ed White, Lakewood Boat Company, Seattle, Washington
Length: 50 feet
Beam: 12 feet 7 inches
Draft: 4 feet
Original Power: Twin Chrysler Crowns
Current Power: Twin Norburg Tarpons (gas)
Construction: Fir hull carvel-planked over steam-bent oak frames.
Teak house. Teak interior. Teak and fir decks.
Home Port: Seattle, Washington

SEVEN BELLS

ANDREW HIMES & ALIX WILBER *Seattle, Washington*

IN 1929 R. B. MACBRIDE, the owner of a Dodge automobile dealership in Modesto, California, used a new Dodge Sport Sedan (valued then at $1,985) as the down payment on a boat he ordered custom-built from the Stephens Bros. Boat Company in Stockton, California. However, after seventy years and twelve different owners, the boat had suffered considerably from neglect. Yet today, this same boat has a new lease on life in the Pacific Northwest.

Since buying *Seven Bells* in 1998, Andrew Himes and Alix Wilber have taken the boat through a major restoration—plumbing, electrical, structural, mechanical, and cosmetic. The aft cockpit has a new teak dodger (protective covering) that provides dry open-air seating space while the boat is at anchor or under way. The forward teak decking has been completely restored, with new teak coverings added to the side decks. Up-to-date navigation equipment—including radar, GPS, and autopilot—now makes her as cruiseworthy as the most modern boat. Her Chrysler-Nissan diesels provide efficient reliability, with the safety of noncombustible fuel tanks.

The interior of the boat is finished in varnished teak, wine-colored leather upholstery, and Oriental rugs. Painted gloss white and trimmed in varnished teak, the forward stateroom contains a double berth to port and a single berth to starboard. There is a fully enclosed head forward, with a hanging locker to port and a built-in teak-faced dresser to starboard. The aft cabin, accessed through a companionway to starboard, has the galley to port, separated by a counter from the main salon, which contains facing upper and lower berths (the top berths fold down to create settee backs). The wheelhouse boasts the original teak joinery work, refinished to perfection.

Most boaters today seem to be content with merely boating—getting out on the water, exploring new territory, and enjoying the sun (or, in the Pacific Northwest, whatever weather they encounter).

Classic boat owners, though, are a different breed. To them, preservation and restoration are first and foremost. *Seven Bells* exemplifies the commitment to excellence that these classic owners share.

SEVEN BELLS

Year: 1929
Designer: Stephens Bros. Boat Company
Builder: Stephens Bros. Boat Company, Stockton, California
Length: 43 feet
Beam: 10 feet 6 inches
Draft: 3 feet
Original Power: Twin Scripps F-6
Current Power: Twin Chrysler-Nissan (diesel)
Construction: Port Orford cedar carvel-planked over steam-bent white oak frames. Teak superstructure. Teak decks.
Home Port: Seattle, Washington

MARANEE

JIM & MARGIE PAYNTON *Seattle, Washington*

EVERY CLASSIC WOODEN MOTOR YACHT carries the cultural stamp of its own period: the mechanical inventions of the teens, the opulence of the 1920s, the Art Deco of the 1930s, the atomic modernism of the 1940s. Sometimes all of these overlap—and a good classic motor yacht can sometimes be as layered as a good book in the way it traces the progress of American life.

Chris-Crafts captured the spirit of the 1940s perhaps more than any other consumer product. They represented functional, highly stylish design, beautiful craftsmanship, and the true beginning of production boats. Most of all, they represented speed. As you stand inside the wide aft cockpit of one of these beauties, watching her wake swirl from either side and feeling the thunder of her engines, you know you are leaving behind the leisure of the 1920s and 1930s and moving into the promise of a dynamic modern decade.

Maranee is a classic example of an early Chris-Craft. Her roomy cockpit area opens to the aft stateroom through a sliding mahogany door. The rear, or "sedan," cabin features two single berths plus a full head and large clothing lockers. Her pilothouse is wide and open, surrounded by full-sized windows for 360-degree visibility. Abaft the steering station to port is a comfortable couch with a table. The forward cabin includes a galley to starboard, leading to double bunks with hanging locker and large storage drawers opposite. There is also a second head. Both of her cabins have not only full headroom but a beam width seldom seen in pleasure boats built prior to the early forties. This is due in part to the rather narrow outside deck space fore and aft and in part to the wider hull design below the waterline.

Owning a Chris-Craft had always been Jim Paynton's dream. He grew up in small wooden boats, and his father, a lifelong boating enthusiast, introduced him to every aspect of the hobby, from piloting and navigation to woodworking and maintenance. Eventually,

Paynton entered into partnerships with his father in smaller cruising boats, but he always wished for full-sized luxury.

"Often we would see a lovely older Chris-Craft double-cabin cruiser out on Lake Union or Puget Sound, and we'd talk about what a perfect family boat such a vessel would make: a little over forty feet long, twin engines, two staterooms, two heads, gorgeous woodwork inside and out."

The dream turned into reality when Paynton discovered *Maranee*, partially wrapped under tarps and waiting to be rescued. Built in Michigan and originally named *Sunny Dee*, she had served as a patrol boat on the Great Lakes during World War II and then had fallen into neglect. Eventually she had been purchased by Wayne Quinton, of Seattle's Quinton Instrument Company, and shipped to the Northwest by rail in 1959. Her current name comes from a combination of Latin and Swahili words meaning "sea princess."

When Paynton found her, most of her exterior brightwork had been painted over. Her interior had been neglected, and all her systems were

in dire need of work. But she represented everything Paynton had dreamed about. So he began a complete restoration, which is still ongoing. He stripped all exterior paint and varnish to bare wood and refinished everything, upgraded the plumbing and electrical systems, and completely refurbished the interior.

Today it's a delight to spot *Maranee* at a classic boating event or cruising the waters of Puget Sound, still powered by her original Hercules engines. Her cabins, restored to perfection, are resplendent with the fine mahogany joinery work of the early Chris-Crafts. Her steering station contains all the original chrome fixtures and instrument gauges. Her floral carpeting is the perfect reflection of a period of palm-tree pins and rattan furniture. *Maranee* is once again a true classic, signaling the end of an old era and greeting a new.

MARANEE

Year: 1940
Designer: Chris-Craft
Builder: Chris-Craft, Algonac, Michigan
Length: 42 feet
Beam: 11 feet 6 inches
Draft: 2 feet 9 inches
Original Power: Twin Hercules (gas)
Current Power: Same
Construction: Mahogany over oak. Double-planked bottom.
Home Port: Seattle, Washington

ISLAND RUNNER

DOUG & RAYMA MERY *Port Townsend, Washington*

PORT TOWNSEND, WASHINGTON, has become the land of promise for thousands of wooden boat enthusiasts annually. Each September this historic seacoast town plays host to the Port Townsend Wooden Boat Festival—a week of intense wooden boat workshops, seminars, and events such as a regatta and a boat show. Year-round, there are courses in every aspect of boat building and wooden boat maintenance. Alive with shipwrights and modern-day facilities for any type of construction, reconstructions, or restoration imaginable, Port Townsend is generally considered the hub of wooden boat activity on the West Coast. One can think of no better town west of Mystic Seaport, Connecticut, in which to own and keep a wooden boat. Doug and Rayma Mery, living in Port Townsend and owning a classic wooden motor yacht, are indeed to be envied.

One of the true Lake Union Dreamboats, *Island Runner* was built by Lake Union Drydock Company of Seattle in 1929 and shipped directly to a company in Wilmington, California, called Yacht and Motor Sales. Over the next sixty years of her life, she had more than fifteen different owners and several different names before the Merys discovered her in 1989 and brought her home to Washington State two years later.

The interior space of *Island Runner* is Dreamboat specific. Her long cabins forward contain the galley, head, dinette, and berths. Her steering station aft opens to covered deck space providing both versatility and comfort. Very little about the boat has changed, but certain things like the queen berth installed in her forepeak and the extension of a hardtop to cover her aft deck have improved the boat's design for use in the Pacific Northwest.

Much of *Island Runner*'s charm comes from her tasteful interior. Fine joinery work, using a variety of exotic woods, creates a rich, warm interior. Teak cabinetry throughout the boat is detailed to perfection.

The brass sink fixtures and wash basin in the head make an otherwise routine area of the boat outstanding. Upgrades to the galley make extended cruising more pleasant.

Since moving the boat to Port Townsend, the Merys have fully upgraded her electrical systems, extended the hardtop, added a swim platform, and re-canvased the foredeck. They have replaced fifteen floor timbers and sistered twenty-three frames, in addition to installing new butterfly hatches, toe rails, rub rails, and a new transom. For a wooden lady who has reached the distinguished status of septuagenarian, few prospects could be healthier than living out her stately years in Port Townsend.

ISLAND RUNNER

Year: 1929
Designer: Otis Cutting
Builder: Lake Union Drydock Company, Seattle, Washington
Length: 42 feet
Beam: 11 feet 10 inches
Draft: 3 feet 6 inches
Original Power: Kermath Model 65
Current Power: Perkins 6-354 (diesel)
Construction: Fir planking over bent-oak frames.
Home Port: Port Townsend, Washington

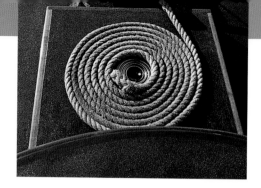

RHINEGOLD

WAYNE HARTRICK, *Vancouver, British Columbia*

BUILT IN 1910, *Rhinegold* IS ONE of the oldest surviving classics in the Pacific Northwest. She is also one of the most nearly original boats of that vintage still in existence. Her current owner, Wayne Hartrick, gives credit for that to a man named C. C. Ferrie.

Colonel Ferrie, as he was known, owned *Rhinegold* for sixty years. Ferrie was a colonel in the Seaforth Highlanders, a regiment of the Canadian Army. He was also active in predicted log racing, which involves the precise calculation of currents, tides, and other factors. As a result, he kept detailed records of everything related to the boat. Apparently, *Rhinegold* was always one of the most important things in Ferrie's life, and as he grew older she became even more important to him. He was known to go down to his boat almost every day.

"According to his family," Hartrick says, "the day the Colonel died he had gone down to the boat as usual, taken her out alone, and caught a salmon, which his wife prepared for their dinner. That evening the Colonel died in his sleep. He was eighty-seven."

From her cockpit *Rhinegold* has the look and feel of a sailboat instead of a power-driven craft, complete with a hard dodger covering the outside steering station. Her narrow beam, long trunk cabin, and mast forward of the steering station all contribute to her sailboat appearance. Below decks, her polished brass lamps and fixtures, gloss-white and deep teak accents, and varnished port-light insets invite admiration. Her detail is exquisite in every way, from the carefully appointed and original galley to the stainless steel Pullman washbasin in the head. As you step in from the cockpit, you enter a cozy main cabin with settee/bunk conversions port and starboard. Forward of the main cabin is a small galley to port, with head opposite. A companionway leads to the forward V-berth cabin, which contains the engine box as well.

Originally built in 1910 for a wealthy British subject who came to Vancouver to manage his family's business operations, *Rhinegold* has seen only two other brief owners besides Colonel Ferrie and her current owner.

"I saw the boat advertised by the man who had bought her from the Colonel's family," says Hartrick, "and I was so impressed by her originality and her excellent structural condition that my partner at the time and I couldn't resist buying her." *Rhinegold* had spent almost her entire life under cover. "It took us five years to restore the boat, which included repowering her with an Isuzu diesel, installing all new electrical and plumbing systems, and taking all paint and varnish down to bare wood. But in all of that, we found very little rot or structural deterioration."

A few things were missing from the boat when Hartrick purchased her, such as the forward skylight and the mast. These had to be re-created

from old photographs. Her original engine, a 1910 Buffalo, was rather massive, which accounts for the engine compartment being placed forward rather than aft. It took up virtually the entire forward cabin, leaving little room for anything else. A smaller, modern diesel now allows a far more functional forward V-berth.

In addition to her racing logs, Ferrie kept all of her cruising logs over the years. "Eventually his family presented me with all of his logbooks," says Hartrick, "dating back as far as 1923. It's amazing, really, to own

something like this. The Colonel cruised the same waters back in the '20s and '30s that we cruise today. I can follow the same routes and anchor at the same coves as he did seventy years before. And no matter where we stop, someone comes up and remarks, 'That's the Colonel's old boat.' And they inevitably have an interesting story to tell about her."

One story reveals a narrow escape. "When the Colonel died, his family members decided to give him a Viking funeral on the *Rhinegold*, and all of the preparations were made. Fortunately, they were denied permission to set the boat afire."

RHINEGOLD

Year: 1910
Designer: Unknown
Builder: Vancouver Shipyards, Vancouver, British Columbia
Length: 36 feet
Beam: 8 feet 6 inches
Draft: 4 feet 6 inches
Original Power: Buffalo
Current Power: Isuzu (diesel)
Construction: Cedar on oak.
Home Port: Vancouver, British Columbia

LAWANA

MALCOM MUNSEY & CONNIE NOBLES, *Seattle, Washington*

THE IMPORTANCE OF *Lawana* in the history of Northwest classic wooden yachts cannot be overstated. As one of the earliest designs by Otis Cutting, she is considered by many to be the "grandmother" of the famed Lake Union Dreamboats.

The frequently misunderstood term "Lake Union Dreamboat," which people often apply to any old varnished wooden cruiser, originated with Cutting. He was a founder of the Lake Union Drydock Company, which became one of the most prominent boatbuilding yards in the Northwest during the 1920s and is still in business today. As the concept of motor-driven pleasure boats was beginning to catch the general public's interest, Cutting (like another Seattle boat designer, Norman J. Blanchard) foresaw the marketing possibilities of a production-style boat.

Based on Cutting's design, Lake Union Drydock Company began building a series of standardized cruisers they called Lake Union Dreamboats. (The term came from a company slogan, "The Boat of Your Dreams.") Dreamboats were usually forty-two to forty-five feet in length, relatively narrow, with a raised deck forward and a covered steering station and seating area—often referred to as a trunk cabin—aft. The raised foredeck provided ample headroom for the cabins and galley below, which were often heated with a cast-iron stove. The covered steering and seating area, which frequently included canvas side curtains, allowed owners to use their boats practically year-round in the mild, albeit often wet, Northwest climate. And Cutting understood these needs as early as 1910, when he designed *Lawana*, which was built by the Taylor and Grandy yard in 1911, before Lake Union Drydock Company existed.

Thanks to their sleek hull design, the Dreamboats could slip through the water with little resistance. *Lawana*'s original engine was only an eight-horsepower Atlas.

Lawana's current structural integrity can be credited in large part to a couple named Gene and Jean Spargo. "They are really the ones who saved this boat for future generations," says current co-owner Malcom Munsey. "They owned her during the '70s and '80s and completed a tremendous amount of restoration, all the while keeping the boat true to her original design and period. In all, she has had eleven owners, including Connie [Nobles] and me." The Spargos did extensive hull and transom restoration. They also extended and enclosed the aft steering and seating area all the way back to the transom, creating a long, comfortable salon.

Lawana's aft cabin, near the waterline, creates a sense of balance and stability less apparent in cruisers with raised wheelhouses. Her lower cabins, perfect for getting out of the cold and wet, begin forward of the steering station with an attractive and original galley to starboard. They lead to a comfortable dinette area with seating or berth combination opposite, in the typical Dreamboat secluded style. Framed pictures, brass fixtures, teak bookshelves, and an attractive green-and-white decor complete these cozy cabins. The glossy white walls and the overhead skylight help make the cabin bright and cheerful.

Owners Munsey and Nobles find the boat quite suitable for two people to live on full time, which they do. "The Spargos lived aboard also," Munsey says. "They were a unique couple, who it would seem lived just to cruise and explore. The logs and the writings they left with the boat tell some amazing tales."

LAWANA

Year: 1911
Designer: Otis Cutting
Builder: Taylor and Grandy, Vashon Island, Washington
Length: 40 feet
Beam: 11 feet 8 inches
Draft: 3 feet 9 inches
Original Power: Atlas
Current Power: Perkins 4-108 (diesel)
Construction: Alaskan cedar over oak frames.
Home Port: Seattle, Washington

ORBA

STEPHEN & YURIYO MOEN & KENNETH MOEN *Seattle, Washington*

HER EXQUISITE LINES AND CLASSIC Lake Union Dreamboat style draw a crowd at any dockside gathering. This beautiful forty-two-foot cruiser has had only three owners since 1927, and that's largely why *Orba* is still so original. Her long forward cabin, typical of the Lake Union Dreamboat layout, includes the chain locker and storage forward, followed by a sleeping compartment. A second salon/sleeping compartment leads to the galley. Up a few steps is the steering station, with a dining area/salon combination and full 360-degree visibility. A sliding front window here permits quick access to the forward deck. *Orba* is that unique blend of cozy cabins down below and bright, airy lounging aft. Her dining area affords lovely views of those endless late-summer sunsets when she is anchored in remote San Juan coves.

Orba was built in 1927 by the Lake Union Drydock Company for Kelly Price, a wealthy stock investor in an oil well company named *Oregon Ba*sin—hence her unusual name, *Orba*. According to current co-owner Steve Moen, her second owner was an inventive University of Washington engineering professor named B. T. McMinn. McMinn designed and built one of the first autopilots ever installed in a pleasure cruiser. It's still on the boat and it still works, after more than five decades. He also designed and installed a refrigeration system that is belt-driven off the engine so that it needs no electrical shore power. Two small homemade tanks produce ice blocks as needed. "I still use it every summer," says Moen.

Other than being repowered in 1965 with a Chrysler Crown gas engine, *Orba* is original in almost every aspect (although Moen has installed a shower next to the head where there had been a hanging locker). He has cruised this elegant yet practical yacht as far north as Johnstone Strait in British Columbia.

<u>ORBA</u>

Year: 1927
Designer: Otis Cutting
Builder: Lake Union Drydock Company, Seattle, Washington
Length: 42 feet
Beam: 11 feet 6 inches
Draft: 3 feet
Original Power: Kermath
Current Power: Chrysler Crown (gas)
Construction: Alaskan cedar over 2-inch oak frames.
Honduras mahogany house.
Home Port: Seattle, Washington

SPINDRIFT

DAVID & HEATHER ELLIS
Seattle, Washington

DURING THE LATE 1930s, Marvin S. Allyn began preparations for his one-year position as commodore of the Seattle Yacht Club by commissioning Ed Monk, Sr., to design the "perfect" fifty-foot motor yacht, *Spindrift*. Allyn chose the Shain Manufacturing Company, one of several small early boatyards on Seattle's Lake Union, to build her. (Shain's official title for the model was "Commodore Trimmer Ship.") According to lore, Allyn would frequently have breakfast with the company's owner and master carpenter, M. G. Shain, to hammer out construction details. *Spindrift* is believed to be the first Monk design built by Shain. (She is also reported to have been the first Seattle yacht taken for military service in World War II—on December 13, 1942.)

A classic motor yacht aficionado coming across several Monk boats of the late 1930s at a Pacific Northwest rendezvous would readily recognize such similarities as their big windows, their long, low-to-the-water design, and the "back porch" coverings over their aft cockpits. In fact, a casual observer seeing *Spindrift* moored next to *Wahoma* and *Rita* might assume that they were all early production models, similar in that respect to the Blanchards and the Lake Union Dreamboats. Yet these three boats were built by three different yards, and once aboard the viewer would easily spot their differences.

Spindrift's uniqueness begins in her aft salon. Like *Wahoma*, she has two large dinette booths to port and starboard, but her galley stretches the beam of the boat abaft the seating area and just before the aft cockpit, so the cook can serve guests in the cockpit, the dining area, or both, just an arm's-reach away.

The feature often referred to by classic buffs as Monk's "big window" design is typical of his consideration for liveaboards, providing excellent natural interior lighting (from large windows rather than tiny round port-lights) and full-view seating arrangements throughout the

boat. *Spindrift* displays this feature, but unlike similar Monk boats, she also includes large aft-bulkhead windows, a unique feature in any pre-war classic cruiser, creating still more interior light and even better viewing for passengers seated in the salon.

And, unlike her counterparts, *Spindrift* has a center companionway leading from the aft salon to the wheelhouse, giving her a "walk-through" interior feel. In fact, one can stand amidships in the salon and look out either beyond the stern or forward of the bow—an amenity uncommon in boats of this era.

Spindrift's current owners, Dave and Heather Ellis, take classic boating seriously. Before discovering *Spindrift*, they were the fortunate owners of *Patamar*. Like many classic lovers, the Ellises spend much of their time researching their boat's history, and they scour swap meets and nautical antique stores for period-specific accessories. *Spindrift*'s galley is graced with antique brass lamps and brass serving ware. The wheelhouse sports a collection of antique brass binoculars and hailers. Exterior bronze and brightwork are detailed to an impressive standard of perfection. Dave Ellis, who keeps his classic inside a fully enclosed boat shed, admits he works on her exterior year-round.

The Ellises are only the fourth owner of the boat, and this is part of the reason *Spindrift* is so completely sound and true to her original design, except for the change from Chrysler Crown engines to her

current Palmers. "Her third owner," according to Dave Ellis, "was R. D. Abendroth, a major partner in Time Oil. He purchased the boat in 1960 from A. Linus Pearson, who had only owned her for three years. *Spindrift* was subsequently held by a brokerage firm and unfortunately kept outside for a year before we rescued her."

Spindrift's original owner was so discriminating that he commissioned one of Seattle's great naval architects to design the "perfect" boat, and guided the builder almost daily while she was under construction. *Spindrift*'s current owner is so dedicated that he keeps her inside year-round—and laments the fact that she once had to sit outside for one year.

SPINDRIFT

Year: 1939
Designers: Ed Monk, Sr., Morris Shain, and Marvin S. Allyn
Builder: Shain Manufacturing Company, Seattle, Washington
Length: 50 feet
Beam: 12 feet 3 inches
Draft: 3 feet 4 inches
Original Power: Twin Chrysler Crowns
Current Power: Twin Palmers (gas)
Construction: Cedar planking over oak frames. Teak house.
Home Port: Seattle, Washington

NONCHALANT

JIM MITCHELL & KATHERINE BELLOWS *Seattle, Washington*

DURING THE LATE 1920s, a Vancouver shipbuilder named Henry Hoffar enticed William E. Boeing, Sr., into expanding the growing Boeing Aircraft enterprise into Canada by becoming the owner of Hoffar's shipyard in Vancouver. Boeing entered the Canadian pleasure-craft market enthusiastically by producing several medium-sized yachts during the 1930s, including *Hulakai* and *Nonchalant*. However, yacht sales were very slow because of the Depression, and both boats went unsold for several years. Hoffar used *Nonchalant* for a time as his family's personal boat before she was eventually purchased by a buyer from the States. Her original asking price was around $7,500 Canadian—which included dishes, monogrammed place settings, bed linens, and a one-hundred horsepower Hall-Scott gas engine. Hall-Scotts, with their six cylinders in line and a piston stroke of seven inches, were famous for their speed, powerful reliability, and quiet operation. Now considered collectors' items, Hall-Scotts were comparable to Rolls-Royce engines in their day, and they were used to power everything from commercial buses to armored tanks in World War II.

Nonchalant's first owner kept her in Everett, Washington, until the 1950s, when she was purchased by a Californian, who cruised her from Everett to San Francisco. Today, when a modern fifty-foot power pleasure boat comes equipped with every imaginable piece of electronic equipment for navigation and safety, few owners would attempt such a voyage offshore, instead choosing to send their boat by truck. In the 1950s, *Nonchalant* would have had a compass—and possibly a radio.

The 1980s saw *Nonchalant* under the ownership of George and Joyce Homenko, who completed major restorations, including replacement of the transom knee, several ribs and planks, fuel and water tanks, and all electrical and plumbing systems.

Nonchalant's interior layout is typical of the Ed Monk, Sr., design for a family cruiser. The forward cabin, which has been remodeled carefully to the original style, contains a double berth with two hanging lockers, a drawer locker, and a small settee. Her raised pilothouse, with engine room underneath, leads to a galley forward of the main salon. Of particular note are her rich teak interior joinery work and original bronze cabinet and lighting fixtures.

The exterior lines of *Nonchalant*, with her raked cabin front and gently swooping cap rails to the lower side decks, are further Monk trademarks. Her yellow Alaskan cedar decks and her amber teak superstructure create a striking color harmony.

Her current owners, Jim Mitchell and Katherine Bellows, discovered *Nonchalant* in 1998, for sale through the Internet. "We sold our Seattle home," Mitchell says, "with the intention of buying a boat to live aboard. It took us several years to find the right one. After searching boathouses and marinas from Canada to California, we finally located *Nonchalant*."

NONCHALANT

Year: 1930
Designer: Ed Monk, Sr.
Builder: Boeing Aircraft of Canada Limited,
Vancouver, British Columbia
Length: 50 feet
Beam: 11 feet
Draft: 4 feet 6 inches
Original Power: Hall-Scott Invader
Current Power: Gray Marine (diesel)
Construction: Yellow cedar over oak frames, fastened with Swedish
iron nails. Alaskan yellow cedar decks. Solid teak house.
Home Port: Seattle, Washington

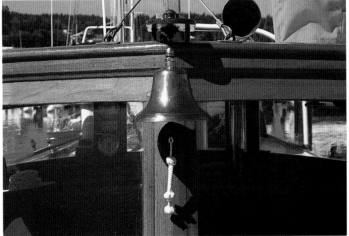

CLASSIQUE

PETER ADEN
Seattle, Washington

Classique's LONG AND STABLE LIFE began back in 1929 in Stockton, California, where she was built by the Stephens Bros. boatyard for a wealthy San Francisco stockbroker named Phillip Finnell. Originally named *Marphil*, she was one of four boats built to the same design for ocean racing between San Francisco and Santa Barbara; her twin Scripps six-cylinder, two-hundred-horsepower gas engines moved her through the water at more than twenty knots.

Her hull, clearly designed for speed, resembles from a distance the hull of a speedboat, with an exceptionally expansive foredeck, and a teak wheelhouse and trunk cabin instead of open cockpits. Yet her "need for speed" is a craving of bygone days, and a tribute to the integrity and practicality of this classic wooden motor yacht is that, after some seventy years afloat, she now functions as the full-time home for her current owner, Peter Aden.

Classic liveaboards like Aden are a unique breed. Because they provide a marina with stability and vigilance, other boat owners always hold them in high regard. A common attitude at any marina is that you are lucky if you have liveaboards on your dock finger.

Classique's liveaboard features begin in her forward cabin. Originally it contained facing settees that converted to berths, with a drop-leaf table in the center, but at some point in *Classique*'s history the port side was converted to a four-place dinette. The galley favors starboard, with entry to the wheelhouse opposite. A unique feature of the wheelhouse is the double-hinged teak doors on either side. Her aft stateroom contains two single berths and a built-in dresser. Unusual for boats of this vintage and design is the fact that the trunk cabin has no companionway leading to the aft deck; *Classique*'s only entranceways are through the side doors of the wheelhouse.

A shipwright and a professional photographer, Aden admits that his original intention was to build a schooner to live on. However, a friend suggested that in the meantime he find a boat to purchase and live aboard while building the sailboat. "As a shipwright," he says, "I went looking for a boat that was sound, functional, and very original. Also, one that was quality-built to begin with."

Classique easily met those requirements.

CLASSIQUE

Year: 1929
Designer: Stephens Bros. Boat Company
Builder: Stephens Bros. Boat Company, Stockton, California
Length: 42 feet
Beam: 10 feet 5 inches
Draft: 3 feet
Original Power: Twin Scripps F-6
Current Power: Twin Detroit 353 (diesel)
Construction: Port Orford cedar. Tough oak frames. Teak superstructure. Teak aft decks.
Home Port: Seattle, Washington

WILLOBEE G

DAVID SEKSTROM, *Seattle, Washington*

FEW SURVIVING CLASSICS IN THE PACIFIC NORTHWEST can match the distinctive interior appointments, the functional exterior design, the antique instrumentation, and the absence of modernization that the *Willobee G* presents to anyone lucky enough to step aboard this beautiful teak and mahogany cruiser.

The wheelhouse, still appointed with the original burnished bronze and brass levers, binnacle, gauges, and wheel, promises more period treasures below. Exquisite teak joinery throughout the interior, complemented by subtly positioned hand-carved fish and various nautical figures, confirms that this vessel is a one-of-a-kind work of art.

The deep, roomy combination galley and dining area is reached by a center companionway from the pilothouse. This cabin, with long settee/bunk combos both port and starboard and a long dropleaf center table, is rich in deeply varnished mahogany. There is a sense of privacy not particularly common in the salon and galley areas of most 1920s cruisers, which typically located berths forward and salon and galley aft.

Abaft the wheelhouse is a second salon, complete with stove and original built-in storage drawers, that can be converted to a stateroom for overnight guests. Aft of this is the large master stateroom, with a double berth to starboard and a roomy head to port. Large bright windows along the bunk make it easy to imagine awaking to the view of a quiet cove or a nearby waterfall.

The name *Willobee G* is derived from the names of the boat's first owners, George Edward Gudewill (Will) and his wife, Beatrice (Bee), who came to Vancouver, British Columbia, from Montreal in 1925. Gudewill, a wealthy manufacturer's agent, had *Willobee G* built for his family in 1927 by the noted Hoffar-Beeching firm but kept the boat for only a year. Like many yachts from the '20s, she seems to have gone through a succession of name changes, owners, locations, and

countries of registration. Although her history is incomplete, it's said that at one point she was traded straight across for a fiberglass Bayliner. Yet somehow she has survived the decades exceptionally well.

"The boat has never been altered in any significant way from the original design," says her current owner, David Sekstrom. "The aft cabin was apparently removed, rebuilt, and slightly widened during the 1930s after a fire, but there are no written records of this. Beyond that, she's close to original."

Willobee G's first engine, a Hall-Scott gas, was replaced in 1935 by a Gardner diesel that is still running well. The deep-well side decks and railings, plus the original outside steering station, make the boat a pleasure to handle in tight situations or choppy waters. Her convenient flybridge steering station is part of her original design. Many classic cruisers of her vintage had this feature added later—often to the detriment of their original profiles.

Under Sekstrom's care, *Willobee G* recently underwent major restoration. Some thirty planks in the hull were replaced, the transom was completely reframed and replanked, and anything else that needed attention was taken care of, buying this important and historic boat many more decades of cruising Northwest waters.

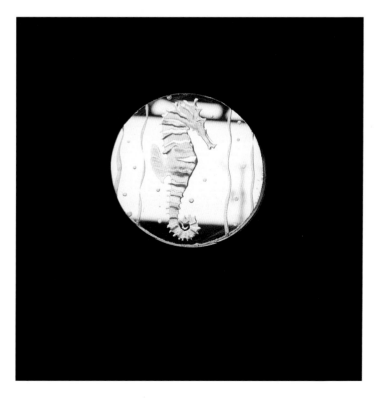

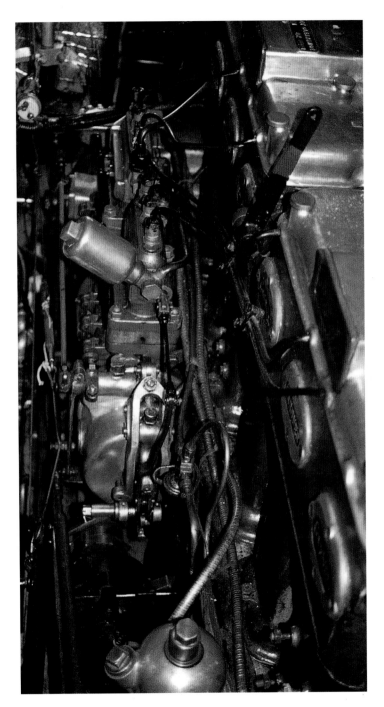

WILLOBEE G

Year: 1927
Designer: Unknown
Builder: Hoffar-Beeching, Vancouver, British Columbia
Length: 48 feet
Beam: 11 feet 9 inches
Draft: 4 feet
Original Power: Hall-Scott
Current Power: Gardner (diesel)
Construction: Yellow cedar on oak frames.
Home Port: Seattle, Washington

GLAYVA

ANDY & JOELLE BLAIR,
CHARLOTTE MacCAY, & TREVOR MacCAY
Seattle, Washington

THE PACIFIC NORTHWEST IS great cruising country. Inland waterways stretch for hundreds of miles from Washington to Alaska, dotted with countless inviting coves and inlets. The coastal climate is mild year-round. Marinas and docking facilities are abundant. And, over the past century, a goodly number of famous naval architects and shipyards have flourished here. It's not surprising, then, that so many classic wooden cruisers still wander Northwest waters. Hidden inside small boat sheds or under covered docks throughout this region are hundreds of classic wooden boats—some as lovely and well preserved as those in this book, others still waiting to be rescued from neglect.

Glayva is one of these well-preserved classics. Built in 1937 in Vancouver, British Columbia, for a man named Frank Reid, she was designed by Tom Halliday, a prominent naval architect of the Fraser River shipbuilding area in Vancouver. Her original name was *Agnes-R I*, and her initial price was a mere $1,160.

Like many cruisers of her vintage, she was pressed into service during World War II: painted gray, she was used by the Canadian Navy as a patrol boat in the Vancouver harbor. Yet, unlike many classic prewar cruisers, *Glayva* was never on the verge of extinction.

"*Glayva* has always been well cared for," says Andy Blair. The boat is owned by Andy and Joelle Blair, Joelle's sister Charlotte MacCay, and her brother Trevor MacCay. They acquired *Glayva* from Joelle Blair's father, Rob MacCay, in 1991. "She has been kept under cover most of her life and never allowed to deteriorate."

Glayva's exterior condition certainly confirms this claim. Her

original Scripps gas engine, which has been faithfully bringing her home for over sixty years." Her pilothouse still utilizes all the original engine controls and gauges.

Glayva appears proudly at nearly every gathering of classic cruisers from Seattle to Victoria, British Columbia. She is a remarkable, if modest, example of the true longevity and reliability of wooden boats built in the early decades of the twentieth century.

canvas-covered decks and pilothouse roof are a gleaming high-gloss white, as are her grab rails, cap rails, and the stanchions that support her varnished teak handrails. Along with her white hull, they create a particularly clean topside appearance, emphasizing the contrast of her varnished teak house and trunk cabin.

The galley includes the original 1933 Coast Foundry diesel stove, still fully functional (and *Glayva*'s main source of heat during winter cruising). "Although her galley was redesigned in the 1950s, and some of the panels in the wheelhouse were replaced, the boat is otherwise original inside and out," says Andy Blair. "She is still powered by her

GLAYVA

Year: 1937
Designer: Tom Halliday
Builder: Mac's Boatyard, Vancouver, British Columbia
Length: 38 feet 3 inches
Beam: 11 feet
Draft: 4 feet 5 inches
Original Power: Scripps (gas)
Current Power: Same
Construction: Yellow cedar on oak frames. Teak house.
Philippine mahogany interior.
Home Port: Seattle, Washington

Cle Illahee

DORIN & UKI ROBINSON, *Seattle, Washington*

THE VISUAL BANQUET OF *Cle Illahee* begins topside, with her original deck fixtures: port and starboard nameplates cast in bronze, a magnificent brass searchlight center forward, a brass signal horn that stretches nearly half the length of her pilothouse roof. Her decks have been laid in beautifully varnished yellow cedar, gracefully following the curves of her hull design. Her sharply pointed bow seats a large, twin-horned bronze windlass—a work of nautical art and the envy of dozens of classic owners.

The sides of *Cle Illahee*'s trunk cabin are marked by exceptionally large round port-lights. Her cabin deck holds a trim lapstrake dinghy to starboard with a swinging davit and a varnished peaked skylight to port. An added luxury is her swinging boom and staysail, which steady her roll through choppy waters.

Cle Illahee is a nautical antique lover's holiday below decks as well. Her pilothouse alone is a dream afloat, filled with polished brass lanterns, brass bells, a huge brass compass, bronze engine controls, varnished deep-red mahogany joinery work throughout, red leather upholstery, books, charts, an antique captain's chair, and a removable mahogany chart table that can easily host lunch for four. Her forward sleeping compartment is one of the few staterooms that are in fact stately. The double berth to port is framed by a carved mahogany stead, and the stateroom is decorated with brass lamps and gilded mirrors of the period. A door leads to the forward head.

Abaft of the pilothouse is a galley stretching the beam of the boat against the center bulkhead. Beyond the galley is her main salon, with settees to either side and a dining table amidships. In all of this interior space, the one overriding impression is that *Cle Illahee* is pure 1920s.

She was built in 1929 by the Vic Franck boatyard, which is still operating today in its original location on the north end of Seattle's

Lake Union. Her first owner was a Seattle judge named Frost, who used her as transportation to and from his summer home in the San Juan Islands. Over her seventy-plus years of plying the waters of the Pacific Northwest, *Cle Illahee* has had the uncommon luxury of two very long-term owners: her current owners, Dorin and Uki Robinson, of twenty-five years, and her previous owner, Milt Benson, who owned her for twenty-three years. According to Dorin Robinson, "This unusual long-term ownership has helped preserve both the originality and the integrity of *Cle Illahee*."

Since buying her in the mid-1970s, the Robinsons have repowered the boat with an Isuzu diesel, updated all systems, repainted her hull, stripped and revarnished her house, replaced several planks, and replaced virtually all of the wood in the stern section. Yet, through all of this, they have always kept *Cle Illahee* completely original. During the 1980s they installed her yellow cedar decks.

Although *Cle Illahee* routinely becomes the centerpiece of any classic boating event she attends, Dorin Robinson is quick to point out that the boat's charm really plays second chair to her cruising capabilities.

"Over the past twenty-five years, we've been in some of the rougher weather Northwest inland waters can offer," he says, "and she has always seen us safely home."

Several years ago when the Robinsons were cruising Desolation Sound, British Columbia, they docked for a few hours in a small Native American village. An elderly Indian man hobbled down and stood for

CLE ILLAHEE

Year: 1929

Designer: Carl Nordstrom

Builder: Vic Franck, Seattle, Washington

Length: 44 feet

Beam: 12 feet

Draft: 3 feet 8 inches

Original Power: Sterling

Current Power: Isuzu (diesel)

Construction: Port Orford cedar planking over steam-bent white oak frames. Mahogany cabin. Yellow cedar decks.

Home Port: Seattle, Washington

some time looking over every inch of the boat. Finally he came up to the pilothouse and asked, "Do you know what *Cle Illahee* means? It means 'Home on the Water.'"

"When I returned to Seattle," Robinson admits, "I looked it up, and he was right. And she's certainly been that for us."

The Robinsons take great care and responsibility in maintaining and improving their classic motor yacht. *Cle Illahee* is a fine example of how a vessel of this vintage can be preserved in her original state while continuing to serve as a functional and enjoyable cruising yacht. Her fine condition has inspired other classic boaters and dreamers for several decades.

ZELLA C

WESLEY & SHARON RUFF
Seattle, Washington

FOR WES RUFF, AUGUST 3, 1967, was a memorable day. "It was my birthday. It was also the day I quit the teaching profession. And it was the day I purchased the *Zella C*!"

It's unlikely that Wes Ruff had any idea of the long-term significance of that day, or that he realized he and his wife, Sharon, would eventually be the owners of one of the most pristine surviving examples of a true Lake Union Dreamboat.

When the Ruffs bought the old wooden boat, she was "a bit of a dog," Wes Ruff acknowledges with amusement. "I estimated her longevity to be five years at most, given her condition."

That estimate is hard to believe now, as you step from the small cockpit of *Zella C* and enter her long main cabin. It feels as though you are standing inside a one-of-a-kind wooden motor yacht recently custom-built for very discerning owners. The floors of the main salon are laid in teak and ash. The wicker chairs, Oriental-style rugs, and polished brass lighting fixtures suggest the 1920s, and the steering station, with its modern navigation instruments and gauges, is in keeping with a restored and updated boat with a '20s motif.

Forward and below are a roomy modern galley to starboard, complete with brass sink fixtures, marble and granite countertops, a built-in teak microwave cabinet overhead, and a large diesel cook stove that keeps the whole boat cozy during winter excursions. The low dining area opposite the galley is warmly surrounded with dark teak bulkheads. The main sleeping compartment, forward of the galley and separated by another teak bulkhead, has a spacious double berth and a large seating area surrounded by additional storage cabinetry. All of the new teak joinery work is clearly the work of fine craftsmen.

A distinctively beautiful solid wooden boat like this, designed and built in the style of the famous 1920s Lake Union Dreamboats, is a rare and marvelous jewel amid today's stock fiberglass production

cruisers. And *Zella C* is the genuine article—one of only a handful of surviving Lake Union Dreamboats anywhere in the world.

"When I bought her back in '67," Wes Ruff recalls, "she literally reeked of a pungent mix of cheap paint, gasoline fumes, musty upholstery, and rot." Ruff wound up using the boat for seven years before putting her up on blocks and building a boathouse over the top of her. At that point, he basically left her in mothballs until he retired in 1986, and the enormous task of total restoration finally began.

"Our first big step was finding the proper woods," Wes Ruff says. After "scouring the entire Northwest" for twenty-foot, vertical-grain, knot-free Douglas fir, the Ruffs eventually found some right in downtown Ballard, a Seattle neighborhood. They bought enough to replank the entire hull. They also found caches of aged teak and stacks of Port

Orford cedar and Sitka spruce and laid in fifty sheets of marine-grade plywood. Then they stored it all to season for a full three years.

The Ruffs built a long-term relationship with a Northwest shipwright named Floyd Waite. Together they replaced twenty-one ribs and replanked the hull, using over five thousand beeswax-coated square-head bronze screws. They replaced all the decks, refinished the cabin with eight coats of varnish, and hand-laid the cabin soles in teak and ash over oak floor timbers.

During this time, Sharon Ruff began researching the boat's history. Up until then, they had no idea about the boat's original name and owner. But in tearing out the stern section, they discovered the name *Zella C* engraved in the planks. That name led them to old Coast Guard documents, a hull number, and the original owner's name: Dennis Cain, of Blaine, Washington. After spending months in libraries and walking the docks asking questions, the Ruffs discovered that "Zella C" was one of eleven aliases used by a popular Northwest madam who at one time owned the La Salle Hotel in downtown Seattle's Pike Place Market. Dennis Cain and "Zella C" apparently were in business together between 1927 and 1930. The Ruffs turned up

evidence that Cain used *Zella C* to run bootleg liquor from Canada during Prohibition and that at one point she was impounded by government agents.

The restoration of *Zella C* eventually became a total reconstruction—hull, stem, stern, and decks; new wiring and plumbing; a one-inch steel keel shoe (thirty-seven feet long and weighing nine hundred seventy pounds), a two-thousand-pound lead cheek, and a new steel rudder; and the new Isuzu diesel. The project took the Ruffs a full decade, but *Zella C* was finally completed and relaunched on May 28, 1997—a full thirty years after Wes Ruff's most memorable birthday. The following year their Lake Union Dreamboat was admitted to membership in the Classic Yacht Association.

ZELLA C

Year: 1927

Designer: Otis Cutting
Builder: Lake Union Drydock Company, Seattle, Washington
Length: 37 feet
Beam: 11 feet 6 inches
Draft: 3 feet 6 inches
Original Power: Kermath Model 65
Current Power: Isuzu (diesel)
Construction: Douglas fir over oak frames.
Home Port: Seattle, Washington

RAGGEDY ANN

LESLIE ASBURY *Seattle, Washington*

IN 1925 A SHIPBUILDER IN TACOMA, Washington, named Karl Rathfon began building small cruisers that he dubbed "Toyships." These boats, designed by Tacoma architect Phillip Thearle, were similar in concept to the Lake Union Dreamboats then being built by the Lake Union Drydock Company of Seattle.

Raggedy Ann (originally named *Wanderer*) was one of the largest Toyships in the Rathfon line, selling new in 1927 for around $2,500. Her layout includes a forward head, a cozy main cabin with a bunk/settee on each side, and a galley. Steps lead up to a Dreamboat-style steering station and aft salon. Her roominess is due in large part to the fact that she was designed with a beam of nine feet six inches. Her lack of side decks adds another two feet of width to the rear salon.

Raggedy Ann's current owner, Leslie Asbury, had the boat's interior restored and decorated to the highest standards of comfort and charm, combining modern features—a microwave, cable television, and contemporary sinks and countertops—with the original varnished teak joinery, bronze and brass lighting, and steering-station controls. Reproduction antiques, period-appropriate curtains, and Oriental carpets, plus a deep, soft leather chair in the salon, create an exceptionally comfortable liveaboard environment.

Asbury works in downtown Bellevue, across Lake Washington from Seattle, and she keeps her boat at a marina on the lake, just five minutes from her office. "I go down to the boat almost every day on my lunch hour," she says. "I take her out every chance I get. The previous owner took her all the way to Alaska, and I plan on doing the same. I only hope that during my watch I can continue to improve the boat as much as her previous owners have."

RAGGEDY ANN

Year: 1927
Designer: Phillip Thearle
Builder: Karl Rathfon, Tacoma, Washington
Length: 33 feet
Beam: 9 feet 6 inches
Draft: 3 feet 6 inches
Original Power: Gray Marine
Current Power: Yanmar (diesel)
Construction: Yellow cedar over white oak, steam-bent frames
with 10-inch centers. Cedar decks with canvas covering.
Home Port: Seattle, Washington

SUNRISE NEW YORK

RUSS & DEE DEE CHERNOFF, *Vancouver, British Columbia*

RUSS CHERNOFF ADMITS THAT IT'S nice to live the dream. "That's what *Sunrise New York* is for us. She's like a tiny paradise that I feel honored to own—whether it's cruising for two weeks in the Gulf Islands, keeping her brightwork up, or just spending an hour or so on her decks away from the office at lunchtime. I feel privileged to have had the opportunity to buy this wonderful boat. For my wife and me, she is a priceless experience that we never tire of. Owning a boat like this is not an investment, it's a passion. A passion that we never want to give up."

Chernoff's feelings are easy to understand once you step aboard the classic yacht *Sunrise New York*. Built in 1930 by the Dawn Boat Corporation of New York City, this boat welcomes guests with an immediate feeling of charm and spaciousness. Classic yachts are noted for their slender physiques and consequently less-than-sprawling interiors. A matter of just a few inches often makes a big difference in interior space. With an eleven-foot, ten-inch beam, *Sunrise New York* seems to find the perfect balance.

Her pilothouse is a roomy, comfortable cabin accented with polished brass and original binnacle and fixtures, a dark-red leather settee that stretches three-quarters of the way across the aft bulkhead, and a beautiful mahogany spoke wheel bearing the manufacturer's name. A center companionway leads forward and below to her guest stateroom—with full headroom and a splendid traditional skylight—which contains bunks, more deep varnished mahogany, and still more brass lamps and fixtures.

The galley and head lie immediately aft of the pilothouse. Beyond that is the main stateroom, with a settee/bunk combination to starboard, complemented by a marvelous period stove and

perfect Art Deco carpeting. Her traditional bridge-deck layout creates that unique feeling of separated space often lacking on modern boats of equal length.

Back in the 1970s, Russ and Dee Dee Chernoff lived aboard a 1929 bridge-deck cruiser for four and a half years, but eventually, as their family grew, they moved ashore. Twenty years later, with the children grown and in college, they began searching for another classic cruiser. They wanted something they could maintain but also spend time enjoying, not something that would require a total restoration. After a chain of disappointments, they saw *Sunrise New York*.

"She was at the Victoria Wooden Boat Festival," says Russ Chernoff, "but she wasn't for sale. Then, a year later, we saw her advertised. I guess it was at that point that we actually started living the dream."

As soon as the Chernoffs purchased *Sunrise,* they began extensively researching the boat's history, gathering a wealth of documents and magazine articles from the early 1930s. In New York City, where she was built, Russ Chernoff discovered that she was one of the last in a line of limited production yachts built for wealthy New Yorkers in the Roaring Twenties. Her first owner's name was B. K. Stevens. Stevens bought the boat in 1930, the year after the stock market crashed, paying $16,900 for her. After a series of owners and a stint with the U.S. Coast Guard during World War II, *Sunrise* was shipped to Portland, Oregon, in 1946 and eventually was brought to Seattle. In 1994 she was purchased by two Canadians named Terry and Cindy Bubb. Vancouver, British Columbia, has been her home ever since.

In his research, Russ Chernoff found several old photos of the boat. "It's amazing how little she has changed over all these years and different owners. And of course that's all part of the beauty of this vessel, part of the mystique of owning a little ship like her—part of a different world, really. When I step onto *Sunrise,* I can leave everything else behind me."

SUNRISE NEW YORK

Year: 1930
Designer: Chris Nelson
Builder: Dawn Boat Corporation, New York, New York
Length: 45 feet 6 inches
Beam: 11 feet 10 inches
Draft: 3 feet
Original Power: Twin Lathrops
Current Power: Twin Ford Lehmans (diesel)
Construction: Cypress over oak frames. Honduras
mahogany house and interior.
Home Port: Vancouver, British Columbia

PATAMAR

KEN & JANE MEYER &
LAWRENCE & SHARON KRAMIS, *Seattle, Washington*

PHOTOGRAPHS OF *Patamar* can be deceiving. Pictured by herself, whether at anchor or cruising, she resembles any of the trim bridge-deck prewar cruisers that still churn Pacific Northwest waters. But in person, she's strikingly different.

At only eight feet wide and thirty-four feet long, this petite beauty could easily fit on the top deck of boats like *Taconite* or *Argonaut II*. Parked alongside them, she might be taken for a dinghy—which is precisely what her current owner believes may have been the basis for her design. "*Patamar* is a Portuguese word meaning 'foot messenger,'" says co-owner Ken Meyer. "It's also the term they used for harbor boats that transported crews and supplies out to larger ships anchored off at smaller ports."

The deception of her size continues when you step aboard this little boat. You quickly discover she lacks nothing that larger cruisers afford. She has ample headroom in the wheelhouse and salon, excellent storage, a roomy and functional galley and head, and a comfortable lounging area in the aft salon. Her interior layout is traditional, with chain locker and small cabin forward, followed by the wheelhouse, with original steering station backed by a large, comfortable settee that converts to a double berth. Aft through a companionway are the galley and the head, and then the main salon, with seating/berths on either side. Steps lead up to her cockpit, and, like most boats of this period, she carries her dinghy on the roof of the salon.

Patamar's charm goes far beyond her size, however. Inside and out, her original condition is evident. Maintained to perfection, she has never been altered in any obvious way.

Because of her size, Meyer points out, he can handle *Patamar* alone in most situations, including coming into and leaving the boat shed—an advantage that any owner whose moorage has a tricky entry path would truly appreciate.

PATAMAR

Year: 1937
Designer: Jake Farrell
Builder: Carr and Stone, Seattle, Washington
Length: 34 feet
Beam: 8 feet
Draft: 2 feet 6 inches
Original Power: Studebaker
Current Power: Chevrolet 292 (gas)
Construction: Cedar over oak frames. Teak house.
Home Port: Seattle, Washington

ARGOSY

RICK & JACKIE ETSELL, *Seattle, Washington*

ONE DAY IN 1934 IN TACOMA, Washington, Dr. Edward A. Rich, an orthopedic surgeon, commodore of the Tacoma Yacht Club, and owner of the sixty-five-foot *Argosy,* topped off both of the yacht's gas tanks and climbed aboard, accompanied by a mechanic. The mechanic smelled gas, but Rich scoffed at his warning and lit a cigarette. The nervous mechanic hastily left the boat. Fifteen minutes later a tremendous explosion killed the good doctor and sank *Argosy.*

Nine years earlier, Rich had commissioned the respected J. Murray Watts of Philadelphia to design the boat based on Rich's requirements. She was built at Edward E. Johnson's boatyard in Tacoma and launched in 1925. In the ensuing years, Rich used the boat extensively, cruising to Alaska every two summers. Rich was also one of the organizers of the famous Capitol to Capitol race from Olympia, Washington, to Juneau, Alaska, a distance of nine hundred eight miles. The race was designed to test the navigational skills of skippers as well as the performance and reliability of their boats. Ten boats participated in the first race, held in 1928, including *Argosy,* who came in fourth overall.

The same year that *Argosy* exploded and sank, Elliott Higgins and his son, Elliott Higgins, Jr., were planning to build a boat for living aboard and cruising to Alaska. They came across the salvaged hull of *Argosy* and saw the opportunity to save time and money. The purchase price was $350. The younger Higgins, a mechanical engineer with a background in naval architecture, began the task of laying out a completely new arrangement of the boat. The result is *Argosy*'s current configuration.

Jensen Motorboat Company on Seattle's Portage Bay began the rebuild, but before it was completed Higgins, Sr., sold the boat to a man named John Wilson, who finished the work. After Wilson's death in 1941, his wife turned the boat over to the U.S. Coast

Guard for the duration of World War II. *Argosy* then worked as a charter vessel between Anacortes and Alaska for thirty-three years. Retired from the charter business in 1978, she had two other owners before Rick Etsell and his wife, Jackie, purchased her in the mid-1990s.

Argosy's current layout includes a spacious and fully covered fantail stern deck, ideal for viewing the passing scenery or dining while at anchor. The cabin top of her aft stateroom is just hip high, making the perfect large banquet table and/or additional lounging area, and it can also function as an outdoor sleeping space on warm nights. *Argosy*'s side decks afford a safe and comfortable covered passageway forward to the central cabin as well as the wheelhouse. The extended top deck over her fantail and side decks provides a platform for two or more dinghies.

Her aft stateroom is accessible from the aft deck as well as through a forward companionway that leads up to her main cabin. The main cabin has been designed as a comfortable dining room/living room/galley, with large picture windows port and starboard. Forward and up, via a companionway to starboard, is the wheelhouse, with large windows overlooking her long forward deck. Crew and/or guest staterooms are below in the forecastle.

The Etsells are carrying out a complete restoration of *Argosy*'s interior as well as major structural repairs, including substantial planking and frame replacement. A naval architect, Rick Etsell admits he "had no illusions that the project would be easy." Keeping tarps in place through Seattle winters is not fun, he points out, and the time and money planned for each task is never enough—not to mention the time and money needed for the unplanned tasks.

"What makes it all worthwhile," Etsell says, "is being able to cruise on a classic from the golden age of motorboating. Efficiency, style, grace, and classic beauty. These boats had it all."

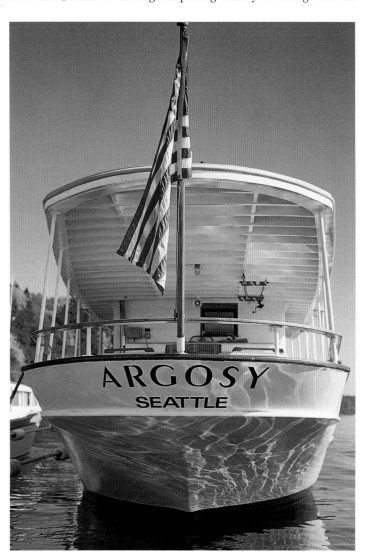

ARGOSY

Year: 1925 / 1938
Designer: J. Murray Watts / Elliott Higgins, Jr.
Builder: E. Johnson / Jensen Motorboat Company,
Seattle, Washington
Length: 65 feet
Beam: 14 feet
Draft: 4 feet 6 inches
Original Power: Twin Western/Wright
Current Power: Twin Gray Marine 671s (diesel)
Construction: Douglas fir on oak frames. Teak decks.
Home Port: Seattle, Washington

DANAE

LESTER & ELIZABETH GUNTHER *Friday Harbor, Washington*

IN 1992 LES AND ELIZABETH GUNTHER attended an international boat gathering at Douarnenez, at the northwestern tip of France, that attracted over three thousand historic wooden boats of every size and type imaginable. "Some of the boats there were over two hundred fifty years old," Les Gunther says, "and all of them looked like boats! I knew then that what I truly wanted in a boat was a classic wooden yacht. So I sold the twenty-four-foot plastic catastrophe I'd bought when I retired, and went looking for a boat with which I could have a love affair."

Danae is the result of that quest, a forty-foot bridge-deck cruiser designed by L. E. "Ted" Geary of Seattle and built at the Vancouver Shipyards in British Columbia. Geary, one of the Pacific Northwest's premier naval architects during the '20s and '30s, was noted for his genius at both designing quick, sleek sailboat hulls and skippering them. Clearly in the Geary style, *Danae* has a slim, semi-displacement

V-hull, easily moved through the water by her current one-hundred-fifty-horsepower Ford Lehman diesel. The exceptionally large windows of her wheelhouse and trunk cabin provide 360-degree visibility.

Danae's interior is both functional and attractive. In addition to a V-berth, her forward cabin also has an upper bunk to port. In the pilothouse, two comfortable cushioned seats abaft the steering station let passengers share the captain's view. A center companionway leads to the galley/salon combination. This main cabin is cozy and attractive, with dark teak bulkheads, dark red upholstery, and curved deck beams overhead.

Les Gunther discovered *Danae* for sale in Sidney, British Columbia. Although her brightwork was peeling and her paint was shabby, she was in good structural condition. The Gunthers have stripped and replaced all her varnish and paint, rewired her, and updated all her electronics. They have also installed or updated various other systems—

forced-air heat, reserve hot water tanks, modern fuel and oil filters—and completely renovated her forward cabin and head.

While cruising in British Columbia, Les Gunther learned that *Danae* had been built as a commuter boat to run between Vancouver and a nearby island where many wealthy Canadians had homes. Because of her speed, there had always been the suspicion that she had run booze during Prohibition, but in fact, Gunther says, the true smugglers' boats had three engines—one for normal running and the other two for escaping the Feds. "So, as much as I would like to think there was a bit of shade in her past, I'm afraid that *Danae* has always been just a lady."

DANAE

Year: 1930
Designer: L. E. "Ted" Geary
Builder: Vancouver Shipyards, Vancouver, British Columbia
Length: 40 feet
Beam: 9 feet
Draft: 3 feet 3 inches
Original Power: Liberty Aircraft
Current Power: Ford Lehman (diesel)
Construction: Double diagonal cedar over steamed oak frames, copper-rivet fastened.
Home Port: Friday Harbor, Washington

KENSINGTON

STEPHEN WILEN, *Seattle, Washington*

Kensington IS IN MANY WAYS the boat that sparked the writing of this book. She is a true example of a "dream afloat." Her long, sleek, black hull glides through the water with grace and elegance. Her dark Honduras mahogany pilothouse and trunk cabin, and her elegant oval aft cabin, are characteristic of the stately cruisers of the 1920s. To a casual observer in the Northwest, she might look like one of the Lake Union Dreamboats that were designed specifically to spend their lives purring across the placid waters of Lake Union, Washington, occasionally cruising north through Puget Sound— kept under dry, covered moorage, and treated more like a precious musical instrument than a boat. Yet nothing could be less accurate.

To begin with, onlookers usually hear *Kensington* coming long before they see her. Her twin GM 4-71s send out a loud growl that has become the boat's trademark in and around her home port. She was designed by J. Murray Watts, of Philadelphia, Pennsylvania— not for languid excursions but as a powerful and fast racing boat for the Delaware River. She was built in 1924 by Smith & Williams Company Marine and Railway of Salisbury, Maryland, for George S. Cox of Philadelphia, president of the Kensington and Allegheny Trust Company. *Kensington* never saw Lake Union or Puget Sound until she was shipped through the Panama Canal by steamer, arriving in Seattle in 1927.

Moreover, the lines her superstructure displays today are considerably different from those she was born with. Her current owner, Stephen Wilen, explains that *Kensington*'s wheelhouse originally had a less-than-attractive raked front. The Blanchard Boat Company, on Seattle's Lake Union, replaced it in 1931 with the current plumb design. Her aft cabin, or solarium, was added in 1938.

Yet, to see *Kensington* under way, it's hard to envision these changes having ever been made to the boat. Her present superstructure seems perfect for her length and her narrow beam.

Wilen came across *Kensington* by chance in 1982 while cruising near Poulsbo, Washington. "She sat rotting away with a For Sale sign in her window. It was one of those defining moments when you simply know things are going to change for you."

At that point in her life, *Kensington* was truly hurting. She stood out in the open, with tomatoes growing in tubs on her foredeck, paint peeling from her sides, and varnish blistering from her brightwork. Much of her interior had been gutted, but fortunately all of the pieces had been saved; and despite her derelict appearance, her hull and engines were good.

Anyone who has refinished so much as a piece of antique furniture has some idea of the work involved in stripping, scraping, stripping again, sanding, filling, repairing, staining, varnishing, sanding, and varnishing ten more coats to create that lustrous "original" wood finish. Consider doing this to a boat that is fifty-seven feet long and over eleven feet wide. *Kensington*'s restoration process also included extensive wood replacement in all three components of the superstructure,

new canvas coverings for the decks, new wiring, new plumbing systems, a refastened bow section, and removal and buffing of all hardware. "I could go on and on," Wilen remarks wryly.

Her interior has been restored to perfection throughout, in keeping with the style of the early 1920s, and redecorated with antique lighting fixtures, nautical memorabilia, and a collection of antique radios. Her deep forward cabin is accessed by steep steps to starboard. The forward head is tucked back to port underneath her steering station. Aft of the wheelhouse are a galley and a long trunk-cabin salon with seating/berths to either side and a second head. Steps lead up to the oval solarium, with curved doors opening to her side decks.

Her period-perfect interior and her authentically restored exterior have won *Kensington* numerous awards, including Best Restored Power, Victoria Classic Boat Festival, 1989; Seattle Yacht Club Golden Potlatch Trophy for Best Classic Power in the Opening Day Boat Parade four years in a row (1995–1998); and Classic Yacht Association National Flagship, 1996. Although she is anything but a Lake Union Dreamboat in the historical sense of the term, few boats have set more dreams afloat than *Kensington*.

KENSINGTON

Year: 1924
Designer: J. Murray Watts
Builder: Smith & Williams Company Marine and Railway,
Salisbury, Maryland
Length: 57 feet 4 inches
Beam: 11 feet 4 inches
Draft: 3 feet 7 inches
Original Power: Twin Detroit Marine Aero Fiats
Current Power: Twin GM 4-71s (diesel)
Construction: Cypress planking below waterline, Honduras
mahogany planking above waterline. White oak frames.
Honduras mahogany house.
Home Port: Seattle, Washington

FREYA

MICHAEL & NEREIDA OSWALD *Seattle, Washington*

IN 1940 A SEATTLE GENTLEMAN named Albert H. Frey asked Northwest naval architect Ed Monk, Sr., to design a boat that would take Frey to Alaska and back—safely, comfortably, and without having to "buy any gas in Canada." The result was the forty-foot bridge-deck cruiser *Freya*.

"Frey actually used the boat for what she was designed for—cruising to Alaska," says current co-owner Michael Oswald. "The logbooks show he went up there twelve times. One of his favorite stops was Princess Louisa Inlet. In fact, he was an original member of something called the Princess Louisa Society, which was formed to preserve the region."

There's a homey feeling as you climb aboard *Freya* that reaches out and invites you inside. From the swinging pots and pans in her galley, adjoined by a comfy dinette area with large picture windows, to the roomy main cabin/steering station, complete with wicker furniture and Oriental carpet, the boat feels comfortable, spacious, and airy. Oversized windows in the pilothouse and salon—which became known as Monk's "big window" design—were an innovative concept for that time, when cruisers typically had small round port-lights, especially in the aft salon.

Like many of her contemporaries, *Freya* was painted gray during the war years when she served with the U.S. Coast Guard. When Frey got her back from the Coast Guard, he had the boat painted turquoise blue—inside and out.

Mike and Nereida Oswald purchased *Freya* in 1992 from her original owner. Changes had been made over the years, notably to the salon and galley, either during the war or when Frey owned the boat. Now, however, *Freya* is virtually the same as when she was built in 1940. At a classic boat show Mike Oswald met one of the original shipwrights who had built the boat. With the man's help,

Oswald was able to determine *Freya*'s original layout and return her to her original design.

One of *Freya*'s most interesting features is an engine compartment that is completely encased in lead. This not only makes the boat extremely quiet while running but also provides an added margin of fire safety.

Freya has required little in the way of major repairs. The Oswalds

have added new electronics, and rebuilt the exhaust and the transmission, but otherwise they pronounce the boat to be "in great shape."

A commercial airline pilot, Oswald plans to retire soon and begin using *Freya* for the purpose for which she was designed. "The goal is Alaska in 2000. She carries two tanks at a hundred-seventy-four gallons each, and she only burns three gallons an hour. That's quite a cruising range."

FREYA

Year: 1940
Designer: Ed Monk, Sr.
Builder: Tacoma Boat Company, Tacoma, Washington
Length: 40 feet
Beam: 11 feet 6 inches
Draft: 4 feet 6 inches
Original Power: Lycoming
Current Power: Crusader 350 (gas)
Construction: Oak frames. Cedar planking.
Locust and fir keel. Mahogany trim.
Home Port: Seattle, Washington

BLUE PETER

JAMES G. MCCURDY
Seattle, Washington

THE STORY OF *Blue Peter* begins with her designer, the fabled L. E. "Ted" Geary. Geary, born in 1885, grew up in Seattle. He began his formal education at the University of Washington's School of Engineering in 1905, ultimately graduating from Massachusetts Institute of Technology, where he studied marine engineering and naval architecture. Geary was already designing and building small sailboats at the age of fourteen. By the time he was enrolled in college, his phenomenal talents were producing forty-two-foot sailboats, one of which he skippered to win the Dunsmuir Cup for the Seattle Yacht Club. By 1914 he would design and subsequently skipper the legendary *Sir Tom*, which held the Pacific Coast Championship R-class title for fourteen years.

To some West Coast sailing enthusiasts, all these achievements are overshadowed by Geary's creation of the "Flattie," a boat he designed in the 1920s for youngsters to build, sail, and ultimately race. But the Geary phenomenon, which included everything from the eighteen-foot Flatties to three-hundred-thirty-foot wooden cargo vessels, is undoubtedly best represented by his magnificent large wooden motor yachts of the '20s and '30s. These wonderful boats, many still in use, were created for some of the most prominent individuals of the early twentieth century, establishing Geary as one of the premier naval architects of the West Coast and leaving as his legacy the remarkable "Geary style." Perhaps most representative of this legacy are *Principia, Canim, Electra,* and *Blue Peter.* These four boats, each ninety-six feet long and all built by Lake Union Drydock Company of Seattle, remain a tribute to the Geary meld of elegance and seaworthy comfort.

Blue Peter's immense, open aft deck, large enough to have served as a dance floor complete with jazz band, conjures visions of the Roaring Twenties. Stairs lead to the main salon, with solid teak

doors on either side. Below decks and forward, the formal dining room contains a built-in dining table and stationary swivel chairs. The walls host paintings and original lighting fixtures. The galley, situated forward between the dining room and the crew's quarters, has remained original—simple and completely functional. Forward of the galley are the crew quarters, complete with facing bunks and a head, plus a teak ladder ascending to the foredeck. In no part of this very expansive boat has any of the 1920s craftsmanship or refinement been altered. This combination of yachtlike interior elegance, superior workmanship, solid construction (*Blue Peter* was built of the finest Northwest timber, making her capable of going almost anywhere in difficult weather), graceful lines, and well-proportioned superstructure all contribute to the Geary style.

Notable examples of this style are evident from a distance in the graceful shape of *Blue Peter*'s hull and proportional size of her superstructure. The contour of her forward section gently sweeps upward, defined by the curve of her rub rail and placement of her many portlights. This gentle rise continues aft, yet is appropriately less pronounced. The overall curvilinear attitude of her profile is accented by

the shape and the height of her superstructure—which incidentally adheres to her curves. The second story wheelhouse is balanced by her large stack amidships—which doesn't protrude skyward, but rather falls gently to the line of her topside tenders. These subtle elements of the Geary style speak (subliminally perhaps) to the constantly shifting curves of *Blue Peter*'s true environment, the sea and sky.

Blue Peter (the common name of the international code flag for the letter "P," raised twenty-four hours in advance of departure) was built in 1928 for John Graham, a well-known Seattle architect. After suffering investment losses in the Depression, Graham sold the boat to Los Angeles businessman George Machris. Machris kept *Blue Peter* until 1943, when he gave her to the U.S. Army for the war effort.

In 1948 Horace W. McCurdy, the successful Seattle industrialist and maritime historian, heard about a boat to be auctioned off by the Army and sent his son, Jim McCurdy (then in his twenties), to investigate. The boat was *Blue Peter*. The elder McCurdy bought her and began a four-year restoration project at his own shipyard, Puget Sound Bridge and Dredging Company.

Today *Blue Peter* is still owned by Jim McCurdy, who uses her as his family's pleasure craft. She is under the full-time care and guidance of Captain Jim Arbogast, who has been employed by the McCurdy family

since 1981. Thankfully, through the commitment and effort of men like Horace W. McCurdy and his son, Jim McCurdy, as well as that of countless other classic wooden yacht enthusiasts, lovely floating dreams like *Blue Peter* have been saved and returned to their former grace and beauty.

BLUE PETER

Year: 1928
Designer: L. E. "Ted" Geary
Builder: Lake Union Drydock Company, Seattle, Washington
Length: 96 feet
Beam: 18 feet 4 inches
Draft: 9 feet
Original Power: Twin Hall-Scotts
Current Power: Twin 334 Caterpillar (diesel)
Construction: Port Orford cedar over yellow cedar frames.
Teak and mahogany interior. Teak decks.
Home Port: Seattle, Washington

GLORYBE

BETSY DAVIS
Seattle, Washington

Glorybe IS A LITTLE BOAT with a quirky past and considerable luck. She was built back in 1914, making her one of the older surviving classics in the Pacific Northwest, and she began cheating extinction just three years after she was launched.

Charlie Taylor and Earl Grandy, Sr., operated a small boat-building company on Vashon Island, just west of Seattle, in the early decades of the twentieth century, turning out some of the first Dreamboat-style boats in the Puget Sound region. They built *Glorybe* for a well-known yachtsman in Tacoma, Washington, named L. A. Jacox. In 1917 she broke loose from her lines during a severe January storm. She was left pounding on the beach, the storm tearing out six of her planks, twisting her shaft and rudder, and ripping off her companionway door. Towed off the beach by a pair of tugboats to the safety of a Tacoma shipyard, she traveled the entire distance—five miles—completely submerged except for her mast.

Her next owner moved the boat from Tacoma to his summer residence on Orcas Island in the San Juan archipelago. One summer's day she turned up missing from her mooring buoy, and he presumed she had been stolen. Eventually, however, she was found by a fisherman near Point Roberts on the U.S.–Canadian border, quietly adrift and in perfect order.

After several different owners over the next decades, *Glorybe* was purchased by Russ and Anne Hohman of Schwartz Bay, on Vancouver Island. The couple lived aboard with their three children. Longtime Anacortes yacht broker Roy Raphael remembers offering the odd little boat for sale in the late 1980s.

"One of the bulkheads had this unusual small opening cut into it," he remembers, "and I couldn't figure out what it was for. Hohman said his wife made puppets, and one of the ways she entertained their children was by putting on puppet shows. She'd sit

behind the bulkhead, and the portal became the puppet stage."

Part of *Glorybe*'s charm is the fact that she retains her original layout, which in some ways is similar in concept to the Blanchard boats of that era. Her steering station opens to the cockpit. The galley, main cabin, and berth are all forward and below decks, lighted only by small round ports and a skylight. Her narrow beam of just ten feet and her stern shaped like that of a canoe (boats of this design are often referred to as double-enders) show the influence of sailcraft on her design.

Glorybe is currently owned by Betsy Davis of Seattle. Davis cruises the boat locally and attends most classic rendezvous, usually handling the boat entirely on her own.

GLORYBE

Year: 1914
Designer: Unknown
Builder: Taylor and Grandy, Vashon Island, Washington
Length: 36 feet
Beam: 10 feet
Draft: 6 feet 6 inches
Original Power: Eastern Standard
Current Power: Isuzu (diesel)
Construction: Cedar and Douglas fir over oak frames.
Home Port: Seattle, Washington

SPIRIT

JAN & KATHI SKILLINGSTEAD *Seattle, Washington*

EVEN WITHOUT KNOWING ABOUT regional boat design traditions of the early 1900s, anyone admiring *Spirit* at her home port in Seattle would probably bet she was built for a place in the sun. Her one-cabin design, with a large, open steering station and spacious aft cockpit, is in clear contrast to the enclosed and separated cabins of boats built for the cool, wet climate of the Pacific Northwest. And, indeed, *Spirit*, built in 1931, came out of the Merrick Boatyard in sunny Long Beach, California.

Spirit's single trunk cabin is forward, and this, plus the contour of her hull, seem more akin to a sailboat than a cabin cruiser. Yet this modest boat has more grace and charm about her than many cruising vessels twice her size, and she lacks none of the comforts and amenities normally found on much larger boats. Her cockpit is spacious enough for a comfortable outside dining area, yet protected enough by a partial cabin top and additional canvas to allow cruising in wet weather. Entered through a portside companionway, the galley is located starboard with icebox and storage opposite. Her long, single-cabin layout with a settee/berth conversion to port and dinette to starboard leads forward to a head and a hanging locker.

Much of her history is vague, but like many Depression-era boats she changed hands frequently. At one time she was named *Aunt Jan* and lived in San Diego. She found her way north in 1993, and then changed owners twice more before being discovered by her current stewards, Jan and Kathi Skillingstead.

Since purchasing *Spirit* in 1996, the Skillingsteads have restored and refurbished this little ship to perfection. After having her hull recorked and refastened, fuel tanks and bell housing replaced, transmission rebuilt, shaft straightened, galley and salon remodeled with the addition of a new diesel stove, and cockpit floors replaced, they now possess a classic custom cruiser that is the envy of everyone who sees her.

SPIRIT

Year: 1931
Designer: Unknown
Builder: Merrick Boatyard, Long Beach, California
Length: 30 feet
Beam: 8 feet 6 inches
Draft: 2 feet 11 inches
Original Power: Unknown
Current Power: Perkins 4-236 (diesel)
Construction: Carvel-planked Port Orford cedar over white oak
steam-bent frames. Teak decks and house.
Home Port: Seattle, Washington

ARGONAUT II

JULIAN MATSON *Boat Harbour, British Columbia*

IT IS LATE JULY AND THE SKY IS FLAWLESS. Summer has ebbed into its postcard phase as my wife, Kathy, and I travel north to Boat Harbour on Vancouver Island, British Columbia, to meet Julian Matson and photograph *Argonaut II*. We are completely unprepared for the experience that's about to unfold.

It began in the routine manner, with my finding reference to the boat in a small Canadian boating magazine, getting the owner's name and number from an old CYA membership book, then writing a letter or two. Eventually the owner and I talked a few times on the phone. The particularly casual and gracious-sounding gentleman at the other end always seemed both pleased and moderately flattered that I would consider including his boat in my book project. But the travel distance was an obstacle. Boat Harbour was a long way north. Our schedules never seemed to mesh. Once we came within twenty miles of each other, but things didn't work out. I would occasionally ask classic boaters stateside if they knew the *Argonaut II* or had ever seen her. A few people had heard about the boat and they spoke very highly of her.

Final deadlines pushed. My own boat began making her annual demands, loud and clear. The summer flew as usual. Then one night Matson was on the answering machine just to say hello and ask how the project was going and if I might still be coming up sometime. There was something about his voice. Laid-back. Modest and polite. I don't know what I envisioned. A polished classic cruiser in a tin-roofed boat shed. A retired gentleman in light slacks eager to show his yacht. I couldn't have been further from the mark.

Matson is this tall, rangy, blond man in jeans and work shirt, bursting with more energy and enthusiasm and stories and anecdotes about historic boats than anyone can possibly digest in anything less than a lifetime—much less a day. We arrived just after

lunch. Matson drove up and met us not far off the main highway north of Duncan, on the east coast of Vancouver Island.

At that point we begin roaring along winding backroads under eighty-foot cedar trees and eventually reach one of the most idyllic settings I have ever witnessed—Boat Harbour. A small, protected cove with a few dock fingers, several marvelous wooden classics, a host of smaller pleasure boats, a wooden boat restoration shop overlooking the docks, and Matson's house of log and stone perched up on a point under cedars and junipers. The house is a collection of nautical brass, books, charts, binoculars—more like the wheelhouse of a boat, or the setting for a movie with Redford or Costner. Matson is graciously offering refreshments. From the serving counter in the kitchen we have a full view of the entrance to the cove as he occasionally picks up a VHF mike and talks to boats in the area. I get the notion that he controls the entrance to the harbor like some pirate—from his kitchen. At the same time my attention is drawn to a view back down to the docks.

There she lies. Backed in. The closest slip to the hill where the house sits. Long and mysterious-looking with her dark-green hull and varnished teak house. The plumb stem of a working vessel, yet the gentle lines sweeping aft of a fine yacht. The attractive curved front of her teak house sweeps back to a large open deck that is covered by an extension from the wheelhouse roof. The sides of her hull show ten large round port-lights, suggesting the expansive space below decks. Her lines depict that settled-to-the-center character of long wooden vessels afloat for many decades.

Before long we step aboard. My hands are instantly drawn to her teak rails—which must be four or five inches wide—feeling their gentle contours, their shallows and curves after decades of sanding and varnish. I think how nice it would be to write a book just on these handrails, to trace the stories of all of the hands that have touched them. Matson has bounded down an aft companionway, already describing how the dining room had three layers of carpet when he bought the boat in 1970 and the oil from the bilge came up over your shoes when you walked across the floors.

Before I can get my mind off those handrails, we're up inside a small cabin behind the wheelhouse and Matson is fast-forwarding a VCR to black-and-white film footage of the boat lunging through impossible

seas with three-quarters of her hull out of the water as she pounds forward. These are historic shots, taken in the days when the boat was named the *Thomas Crosby IV* and was owned by the United Church of Canada, which serviced remote areas. They were called "Mission Boats," and Matson explains how they were in service fifty weeks a year up and down the B.C. coastline—carrying doctors, supplies, and medical needs, breaking ice, towing barges.

Except for the TV, everything in the cabin appears either antique or in some way historic. A small church pump organ, strange prewar electrical boxes, a unique wood-burning stove, sun-blanched curtains. A small bronze cannon on the floor by the woodbox. There are books everywhere.

The wheelhouse is impossible to process. Antique brass radiators, binnacle, an immense wheel, a colossal antique Decca radar installed in 1954 that still works! (Matson says it is the only one still in existence anywhere in the world that works.) In fact, everything in the pilothouse still works. Everything on the boat still works. Nothing is on the boat merely as a keepsake or a memento of a bygone era. Nothing for show. Clearly Matson's style. Everything that functioned when she

plied the B.C. coastline as a Mission Boat still functions today—including the thirty-two-volt electrical system.

Matson has led us down into the engine room. It's unbelievable. A 1942 air-start Gardner six-cylinder diesel. Polished stainless, polished brass, polished bronze and copper. The sweet smells of oil. A spacious tool room and workbench. I feel I've been hologrammed into some previous dimension. Matson is explaining how the massive hand-crank air compressor eventually turns over three of the six cylinders, which in turn, turn over . . . It's endless.

Abaft the engine room is a galley whose only modern improvement is a diesel cookstove. Beyond that, the main salon with huge dining

table, framed charts, leather sofas, brass lamps, and books and books and books. This is a room of ideas, of lost emotions. Minds struggled here. Hearts cried. There's just too much to take in.

Matson is rambling on about someone named Pirate Kendall and the cannon on the point and how they once had to fire it at John Wayne as he entered the cove aboard his converted minesweeper. Meanwhile he's laying out original journals and accounts of the Mission Boat days and old photos of Peter Kelley, who was her captain for sixteen years and the son of a Haida chief from the Queen Charlotte Islands. Written accounts of how this vessel was a lifesaving link for the isolated canneries, Indian villages, lighthouses, logging and mining camps. How she functioned as a floating hospital, library, post office, maternity ward, church, mortuary. Births. Deaths. Sorrow. *I heard the owl call my name.* How she was originally built as a pleasure yacht for the Powell River Company in 1922 and named the *Greta M.* Purchased in 1937 by the

United Church of Canada and renamed the *Thomas Crosby IV*. In service for thirty years straight until she was sold in the 1960s and allowed to badly deteriorate. Discovered by Matson in 1970. Restored to original perfection over a period of thirty years and counting.

Matson and I have crawled up on top of the wheelhouse roof. I focus on the massive windlass mounted on the foredeck below me, the patina-coated brass searchlight at my feet, the large smokestack behind me. Yet I keep thinking about those wide teak handrails, of all the anxious hands that have held those rails over the decades of service along the rugged B.C. coastline.

It's late. We sit inside a historic English pub for dinner—the first pub ever established on the island. Matson is telling stories about Pirate Kendall, the original owner of Boat Harbour. I can't get the *Argonaut II* out of my mind. The history she carries because she is still

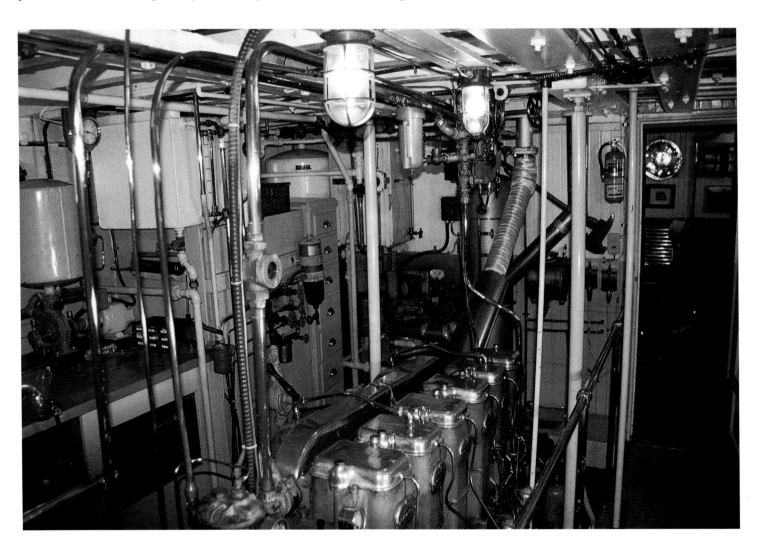

so perfectly original. The endless care Matson has taken to preserve that originality, that feeling, that strange mystique the boat still owns. I suddenly feel anxious to get home and resume working on the restoration of my own boat, rejuvenated about the concept of keeping old wooden boats alive. They are important. Perhaps more important than their owners or stewards.

It's been a strange day. A tiring day. An indelible encounter for both Kathy and me. We drive south toward Victoria in silence. I can't get the boat out of my mind. I have never stepped aboard a more hauntingly magical and spiritually powerful classic, or met a more interesting and gentle character. We'll never forget *Argonaut II*. Or Julian Matson.

ARGONAUT II

Year: 1922
Designer: Edison B. Schook
Builder: Menchions Shipyard, Vancouver, British Columbia
Length: 73 feet
Beam: 14 feet 7 inches
Draft: 6 feet 7 inches
Original Power: Fairbanks Morse
Current Power: 6L3 Gardner air-start 6 (diesel)
Construction: 2½-inch Port Orford cedar, carvel-planked over bent oak frames. Teak house. Fir decks. Gumwood stem.
Home Port: Boat Harbour, British Columbia

GLOSSARY

Abaft: To the rear of; toward the stern from; behind.

Aft: At, near, or toward the stern (back) of the vessel; opposite of fore or forward.

Beam: Width of the vessel.

Boatwright: An experienced ship carpenter; shipwright.

Bow: Forward end of the vessel; opposite the stern.

Bridge: A raised transverse platform on a vessel that holds the steering station and from which the vessel is navigated.

Bridge deck: Covering over the bridge or wheelhouse.

Brightwork: Varnished woods or polished metals; not painted.

Bulkhead: Partition separating cabins or staterooms.

Cap rail: Fore and aft capping rail of the hull, usually supporting stanchions, or handrail posts.

Carvel planked: Planks laid flush at seams, rather than overlapped; flush planked.

Chain locker: Place where the anchor chain or anchor rope are stowed.

Cockpit: A space lower than the deck, usually to hold crew.

Companionway: Entranceway, usually a stairway, from deck to cabin.

Davit: Crane or hoist for raising and lowering the dinghy.

Dinghy: A small boat; tender.

Displacement hull: Full floating; not planing or rising.

Flybridge: An external steering station or upper bridge; additional control station.

Fore: At, near, or toward the bow (front) of a vessel; opposite aft.

Foredeck: The forward deck area, between the bridge and the bow.

Forepeak: The extreme forward section of the boat.

Forward: To or toward the bow (front) of vessel; in front of.

Galley: Cooking room; kitchen.

Handrail: Rail, usually wood, mounted on stanchions or supports; balustrade.

Hanging locker: Storage compartment for hanging clothes; closet.

Hard dodger: Firm covering (e.g., wood or metal as opposed to canvas) over cockpit or outside steering station, protecting the area and the crew from the weather.

Hardware: Metal fixtures or fittings, often brass or bronze.

Hatch (or hatchway): Opening in deck to provide access to below; also covering over a hatchway.

Head: Toilet; bathroom.

Helm: The steering station on the vessel; the steering wheel.

House: Protective housing or cabin, such as a wheelhouse.

Hull: Basic part (the body) of a boat, exclusive of the house.

Joinery work: Skilled woodwork, especially where pieces of wood are joined; the finer woodwork in vessels.

Keel: Main structural member of a boat's hull, running longitudinally along the bottom of the boat.

Knot: Unit of speed equal to one nautical mile per hour; 10 knots is roughly equivalent to 12 statute miles per hour.

Mast: Pole; the principal vertical wooden spar for supporting sails, booms, radio antennas, flags, and so on.

Pilothouse: Enclosed space housing the steering station and navigational instruments; wheelhouse.

Planking: Lengths of wood used for the external skin of the hull or decks.

Port: Left side of the vessel looking forward.

Porthole: An opening in the side of the vessel to admit light or air.

Port-light: The glass in the porthole to keep it weather tight; window.

Rendezvous: Gathering of boats for the purpose of showing to the public; boat show.

Rib: Frames; the transverse timbers of the hull to which the planks are fastened.

Rudder: The flat structure submerged near the stern by which the vessel is steered.

Rudder post: Post holding the rudder.

Salon (or saloon): Usually the main or most comfortable cabin; social room.

Side deck: Deck space running fore and aft alongside the main cabin.

Sister ship: Of the same type in design and form.

Solarium: Glass-enclosed space.

Stanchion: An upright post for supporting a rail or handrail.

Starboard: Right side of the vessel looking forward.

Stateroom: A private room or cabin.

Steering station: Control station or place of the helm.

Stem: The upright continuation of the keel at the vessel's fore end; the post the planking is fastened to at the vessel's forward end.

Stern: The extreme aft end of the vessel; opposite the bow.

Swim step: Additional extension usually added at the stern of the boat to allow ease of boarding from a dinghy or from swimming.

Toe rail: Narrow strip placed on the gunwale, or top edge of hull, to finish it off; also used for safety.

Transom: The transverse, side to side, structural members of the hull at the stern.

Trunk cabin: A cabin having its sides only partially above the deck.

V-berth: A V-shaped berth, forward, that conforms to the shape of the vessel's bow.

Wheelhouse: An enclosed cabin that protects the helmsperson and steering station; pilothouse.

Windlass: A winch, manual or electric, for pulling up the anchor chain or anchor rope.

NORTHWEST WOODEN BOAT FESTIVALS

Following are some of the festivals attended by classic wooden
yachts such as those featured on these pages. For more information about the festivals,
contact the local chambers of commerce, check events listings in marine publications such as
Nor'westing, The Northwest Yachting Magazine Magazine (206-783-8939, www.boatjournal.com) or *48
Degrees North, The Sailing Magazine* (206-789-7350, www.48north.com), or consult the Classic Yacht
Association website at www.sonic.net/~georgeh.

SEATTLE'S OPENING DAY OF YACHTING SEASON
Montlake Cut, Seattle, Washington
Early May. Hundreds of boats—motor and sail, classic and new—
join the regatta from Lake Union to Lake Washington through the
Montlake Cut. Marks the official beginning of the boating season. Crew
races are held in the cut in the early part of the day. Seattle Yacht Club,
206-325-1000.

OLYMPIA WOODEN BOAT FAIR
Percival Landing Park, Olympia, Washington
Early May. Attracts a large number of classic motor yachts, sailboats, and
work boats. Includes free jazz and entertainment, plus nautical exhibits,
booths, and food. 360-943-5404.

VINTAGE VESSEL GATHERING
Maple Bay Marina, British Columbia
Late May. Held at Maple Bay Marina on the eastern shore of
Vancouver Island. Attracts a large number of classic motor yachts,
tugs, and work boats.

BELL STREET PIER CLASSIC RENDEZVOUS
Bell Harbor Marina, Seattle, Washington
Early to mid June. The largest gathering of pre-war classic cruisers on the
West Coast. Sponsored by the Classic Yacht Association.

THE LAKE UNION WOODEN BOAT FESTIVAL
Lake Union, Seattle, Washington
Fourth of July weekend event. Attracts a wide range of wooden classics
ranging from kayaks to tall ships. Extensive booths, workshops, museum
displays, and exhibits at the Center for Wooden Boats on Lake Union.
Sponsored by the Center for Wooden Boats, 206-382-2628,
www.cwb@cwb.org.

ANTIQUE & CLASSIC BOAT SHOW
Gene Coulon Beach Park, Renton, Washington
Late July. Attracts runabouts, launches, pre-war classics. Sponsored
by the Antique Classic Boat Society, www.halcyon.com/pford/acbsx.

VANCOUVER WOODEN BOAT FESTIVAL
Granville Island, Vancouver, British Columbia
Late August. Attrtacts canoes, kayaks, classic power and sail,
work boats, and tugs. Includes workshops, maritime booths, and
Vancouver's Public Market.

VICTORIA CLASSIC WOODEN BOAT FESTIVAL
Victoria Harbour, Victoria, British Columbia
Labor Day weekend festival. Classic sail and power, steam launches, work
boats, and tall ships. One of the largest collections of wooden boats in the
Pacific Northwest.

PORT TOWNSEND WOODEN BOAT FESTIVAL
Point Hudson Marina, Port Townsend, Washington
Mid September. The largest all-around wooden boat festival on the West
Coast, featuring exhibits, workshops, lectures, live music, crafts fair, and
annual fund-raising event to support maritime educational programs for
youths and adults. Sponsored by the Wooden Boat Foundation,
360-385-3628, www.olympus.net/wbf.

Published by Sasquatch Books, Seattle
Printed in Hong Kong
Distributed in Canada by Raincoast Books, Ltd.
04 03 02 01 00   5 4 3 2 1

Grateful acknowledgment is made to the following individuals for providing
photographs for reproduction within this book. All other photographs are by the author.
Jim Arbogast (page 138, *Blue Peter*); Jane Asbury (page 110, *Raggedy Ann*); Tom Bowen (page 74,
Rhinegold); Earl Dodson (page 45, *Charles H. Cates*); Dave Ellis (page 67, *Island Runner*, page 85,
Spindrift; page 89, *Nonchalant*; page 99, *Glayva*); Steve Gordon (page 32, *Hanna*); Elizabeth Gunther
(page 38, *Mahar*); Les Gunther (page 123, *Danae*); Mark Kaarremaa (page 157, *Argonaut II*);
Marty Loken (pages 2 and 47, *Mer-Na*); Mike O'Brien (page 17, *Haida Princess*); Uki Robinson
(page 105, *Cle Ilahee*); Steve Wilen (page 125, *Kensington*); Nancy Wistrom (page 120, *Argosy*).

Cover and interior design: Karen Schober
Copy editor: Alice Copp Smith

Library of Congress Cataloging in Publication Data
McClure, Ron.
Classic wooden yachts of the Northwest / Ron McClure.
p. cm.
ISBN 1-57061-230-7 (alk. paper)
Yachts—Northwest, Pacific. I. Title.
VM331.M39 2000
623.8'2023—dc21
00-021748

Sasquatch Books
615 Second Avenue
Seattle, Washington 98104
(206) 467-4300
www.SasquatchBooks.com• books@SasquatchBooks.com